The
LEARNING MENTOR'S RESOURCE BOOK

A Lucky Duck Book

2nd Edition

The LEARNING MENTOR'S RESOURCE BOOK

KATHY SALTER & RHONDA TWIDLE

Los Angeles | London | New Delhi
Singapore | Washington DC

Second edition published 2011

First edition published 2005

Reprinted 2006, 2008 (twice), 2010

SAGE Publications Ltd
1 Oliver's Yard
55 City Road
London EC1Y 1SP

SAGE Publications Inc.
2455 Teller Road
Thousand Oaks, California 91320

SAGE Publications India Pvt Ltd
B 1/I 1 Mohan Cooperative Industrial Area
Mathura Road
New Delhi 110 044

SAGE Publications Asia-Pacific Pte Ltd
33 Pekin Street #02-01
Far East Square
Singapore 048763

Library of Congress Control Number: 2010924550

British Library Cataloguing in Publication data

A catalogue record for this book is available from the British Library

ISBN 978-0-85702-069-7
ISBN 978-0-85702-070-3 (pbk)

Typeset by C&M Digitals Pvt Ltd
Printed in India at Replika Press Pvt Ltd
Printed on paper from sustainable resources

CONTENTS

A note on the use of gender

Rather than repeat throughout the book the modern but cumbersome 's/he', we have decided to use both genders equally throughout the range of activities. In no way are we suggesting a stereotype for either gender in any activity. We believe that you can adapt if the example you are given does not correspond to the gender of the child in front of you!

A note on the use of the words 'family' and 'parents'

Many children do not live in conventional two parent families. Some are looked after by the local authority and might have confusing and painful experiences. We often use the term 'carer' to identify the adults who look after such a child or young person. Sometimes 'people you live with' might be more appropriate than 'family'. These phrases can make the text rather repetitive. Please use the words most suitable for the young people you work with.

INTRODUCTION

This book is an attempt to bring together resources for the myriad of different areas that Learning Mentors, and others involved in the pastoral care of school students, are required to be able to deal with. It will be of use to teaching assistants, teachers, school nurses, personal advisors and lunchtime staff, as well as Learning Mentors. In fact, many of the activities are useable or at least transferable to a number of different settings in which young people are receiving support, such as youth offending teams, family support teams, children's residential homes, youth inclusion projects, and youth services. The resources are aimed at anyone working with young people from ages 10 to 16 (late Key Stage 2 to Key Stage 4) although some activities and worksheets will work with children either side of this age range and can be adapted to suit.

We first produced this book and its materials when working as Learning Mentors ourselves in a large Leeds high school, having created a great many resources that we used regularly with students. At that time, the books we had available to refer to were limited, although we are pleased to see an increase in pastoral resources. Learning Mentors and pastoral staff needed to provide responses to such a wide range of difficulties that no one resource would cover them all. In the days of tight budgets, we set out with the intention of providing something of a 'one-stop shop' that we hope is at least a starting point for the areas most regularly encountered. We devised the majority of the activities described, but some are derivative of activities we have experienced during years of training days and other interesting events. We have now transferred into different fields; Kathy Hampson is an experienced worker within the Youth Offending Service and is currently completing a PhD and Rhonda Mitchell worked as a Probation Officer, including a secondment with a Family Intervention Project, and is now a Practitioner with the Child and Adolescent Mental Health Service. We believe such experiences have a brought a more holistic context to this edition – and it is worth noting that we have used the resources across all settings!

The paperwork needed to run a mentoring programme in a school will differ depending on the existing processes already underway, like registration methods and the availability of computers for record keeping. We used a variety of paperwork, some of which we have outlined below. For more information on what you might encounter, another good resource is *The Learning Mentor Manual* by Stephanie George (Sage, 2010). Incidentally, it may be a good idea to identify a colour of paper that all your paperwork will be printed on, as pupils and teachers alike can easily identify it, and it may be less likely to go astray! We always used light green – probably as this was the colour of paper that we could find at the time we started!

Register appointment request – we used a slip of paper which the teacher would hand to the pupil. It had on it a form requesting the pupil for an appointment at a certain time in our room. We placed these in registers that were all together at the beginning (or end!) of the day, so they were easily accessible. This also made it easy to find out whether the pupil had received the appointment or not.

Pupil meeting log – we always wrote up our appointments and kept files on all official referrals, while pupils using our break time drop-in were recorded in a book, which was regularly reviewed. This enabled us to remember what was said last time and what was agreed. They can be completed either on the computer as word documents, or on paper in a paper file, if you do not have reliable access to computers.

Parent/carer letter – if pupils are being mentored then their parents or carers need to know about it! We wrote a letter for each new referral giving an outline of our service, what the pupil could expect, the reason for the referral, and contact details for parents to ring if they wanted to know more or access further support from us.

Report sheet – we had our own report sheet with our targets on, and a space for each teacher to rate how much they feel that pupil has achieved in that lesson. There should be no more than three targets. As well as helping you to see what is really happening, it also reassures teachers than something is being done about issues which they have found difficult.

Rewards/certificates – we always rewarded our mentees when they achieved targets, and created bronze, silver, and gold certificates which we printed up on parchment paper. The pupils seemed to really value these, and enjoyed working their way up the range. We had samples on our walls so they could see right from the beginning what they could earn. We found that often our certificates were the only achievements these pupils were making, which made it even more important that we celebrated their successes!

More complete and diverse paperwork examples are included in other books, although you may find they need a fair amount of adaptation to fit your situation.

We have endeavored to cover the most common areas that Learning Mentors encounter in supporting young people and in recognition that new issues do arise in this ever-changing world, we have added two new chapters in this edition to address the issues of Internet safety and hate behaviour. However, it is important to accept when working with young people and their families that you may not be able to address every need they present. This makes knowing about the other agencies in your area very important, as you can then signpost appropriately to them. Some agencies, like Child and Adolescent Mental Health Services (CAMHS) and Social Care, are national, but local working practices may well differ, so find out about local provision. It is a good idea to map the services available in your area (and nationally for some agencies that offer national helplines), so you have at your fingertips the information you need when presented with an issue. Make sure you identify their referral criteria, what information they require, and how they work in practice, as most agencies require agreement on the part of the service user to enable them to accept the referral. This means you can give all the information someone might need in order to make a decision. It is also useful to know whether there is likely to be a waiting list before the family can expect help.

Unfortunately, many voluntary organisations are funded from fixed pots of money, which then dry up, causing the project to fold. As someone interested in service availability, this can be incredibly frustrating, so ensure your list is kept up to date!

The current context

Children's services are now moving more towards the use of CAFs (Common Assessment Frameworks) with young people and their families. This is a method of coordinating the help that is available to address the needs of children, young people, and their families. Anyone who is CAF-trained can initiate one, as long as the family consents and there is more than one issue to be addressed, so if you have not already received some training on this, it would be useful to request it! The CAF model begins with in-depth assessment of the situation, identification and classification of needs, and then a matching of services to address those needs. A meeting is arranged, where each agency who is contributing to the CAF identifies exactly what they are going to do, and this is put into an action plan. The plan is reviewed later and possibly re-drafted to reflect what has changed or identify targets that have not yet been met. It creates more accountability for agencies to carry out agreed actions, and helps make addressing complex needs more attainable. There is sometimes money available to achieve some aspects of the plan, which can be a useful addition.

While multi-agency working has long been part of the Learning Mentor role and wider context of working with children, there is an increasing drive towards integrating the family in such work, so-termed the Think Family approach. The basic premise is that working holistically with family support, rather than from only a school perspective, will have more impact for the young person. If the issue is actually with a parent, then supporting them to address it will be the most effective action. This whole family approach recognises the importance of the child's most immediate environment in addressing deeper or 'social' issues and has resulted in a recent increase in family provision such as Family Intervention Projects, Children's Centres and parenting programmes. The Government expects that from 2010 all schools will provide Extended Services; namely activities outside of school hours for children, families and the local community to access. Extended Services are designed to help balance work and family commitments by offering pre and post school activities that give children the opportunity to engage in a broader range of experiences – such as sports, music, arts – and support academic study. Schools are also encouraged to offer parent support groups and behaviour management programmes. Clearly there is not the space within this book to discuss parenting strategies but one of the most well-evidenced based series of parenting programmes is that established by Dr. Webster-Stratton known as The Incredible Years (www.incredibleyears.com). We would suggest that Learning Mentors explore which programmes are favoured locally and what training is available, particularly if you wish to offer parenting groups as part of Extended Services. Being trained in such groups can also benefit your one-to-one work with children and supporting families individually.

Confidentiality

A word ought to be said about confidentiality. We operated under a strict code of confidentiality, which we displayed so that all students could see it. In this statement we explained that we can keep things confidential (with an explanation of that word!) as long as the student is not being placed, or placing others, in danger. We also did not ensure confidentiality when illegal activities are being discussed (this may not be the case in your establishment – check your own confidentiality guidelines). If this is clear at the start, then all students can make the decision as to whether they tell you personal information or not. It safeguards the relationship with the student, as she will then not feel betrayed if you feel you cannot keep what she says to yourself; however, you must tell her if you need to pass it on, and also be very clear about who will be told, so she knows how far the information will go. In some areas, such as self-harm, it is important to be clear beforehand how much you will keep confidential, and at what stage you feel you need to pass it on for Safeguarding.

Using the Resources

The worksheets and activities presented within this book are generally more effective when used within the context of an appropriate trusting relationship between the mentor and the young person, which is found to be more important for success than the theoretical approach used. Although Learning Mentors are not qualified counsellors (nor are they expected to be), some knowledge of basic counselling skills is essential. We tended to use the style of Socratic questioning, which is an open and guided questioning technique that facilitates the pupil to reach their own conclusion and explore the problem themselves, whilst avoiding the impression of instructing. As most of the worksheets lead on to further discussion with the student, we suggest that you focus on Socratic questions to avoid just yes or no answers: young people can be difficult enough to draw out as it is and closed questions tend to make them clam up more! We would also advise cautious use of the question, 'Why?' as it can be interpreted as being judgemental and too direct. Try to phrase your question in a different way. Young people come to Learning Mentors with sensitive problems and will make mistakes; they do not want to be judged and they need your belief in their ability to change and survive. Using your communication skills to listen and reflect back to the young person will show respect and a friendly, open approach which young people respond to.

Additionally, it is helpful to have a basic understanding of the different theoretical approaches behind the interventions most frequently used. The majority of the worksheets and activities presented in this book are based upon the following different approaches, or a combination. We have provided a brief explanation of each theory but you can refer to the bibliography for more detailed literature.

Motivational Interviewing   focuses on resolving ambivalence to enable change and uses the Cycle of Change model to recognise the process an individual will encounter when changing a behaviour (see Miller and Rollnick, 1991).

Solution-Focused Brief Therapy   was developed by Steve de Shazer and Insoo Kim Berg in the 1980s and concentrates on the person's existing strengths to find solutions rather than dwelling on the problem. This approach is short-term and involves goal-setting.

Cognitive-Behavioural Therapy   basically originates from two psychological approaches: 'Behaviourism' and 'Cognitivism'. Behaviourist theories stress environmental stimuli in determining the actions of an individual while cognitive theories view the internal processes within a person as fundamental in understanding behaviour. Cognitive-behavioural therapy synthesises these approaches and considers the relationship between thoughts, feelings and behaviour as a consequence and predictor of future thoughts. Thus if a person can change their particular thoughts about a situation, this will impact upon their feelings and ultimately their behaviour.

As well as considering our own skills and knowledge, we need to think about the students. Many schools now identify their pupils' preferred learning styles, acknowledging that learning materials are not going to suit every young person in a class. There are a variety of tools available to do this, and there is more than one model of learning style types, although possibly one of the simplest identifies people as being mainly auditory, visual, or kinaesthetic learners. The exercises included in this book can be adapted for different learning styles. For example, a pupil who is an auditory learner may not develop well through the use of worksheets, but those same basic resources can be used in question and answer sessions, discussions, vocal presentation of ideas, or using music and other recorded material to bolster the worksheets. Kinaesthetic learners are more likely to be engaged with a physical activity, so worksheets can be adapted into laminated cards which can be physically categorised, or other activity-based rather than worksheet-based exercises could be chosen. We would actively encourage you to be imaginative in your use of these resources, adapting them to the learning styles and abilities of each pupil as appropriate. Pupils are often in the mentoring room in the first place because their style does not fit well with the accepted norm!

The resources can be used across the chapters for different difficulties, and of course worksheets can be used in whichever way you find most useful. Our guidelines for use are merely what we had in mind when we created them. Each worksheet is printed in the same order as they are detailed in the chapter, followed by suggested activities. We then give combined ideas for helpful contacts and further reading as, more often than not, the contacts also provide reading material and information.

We have labelled each sheet with information that should help you to navigate within the chapters. We have specified the age range it is suitable for, and provided a key to explain what type of sheet it is. There are three types of worksheet:

❗ Information – this is information for the Learning Mentor, other members of staff or parents and carers.

⛁ Student information – these are sheets that contain information for the student, rather than a specific task.

✏ Student worksheets – these are worksheets that contain tasks that the student can complete.

Each sheet is replicated on the included CD-ROM, for your ease of use.

Worksheets

Getting to Know You

Included in this introduction are a couple of 'getting to know you' ideas to help the initial contact with the student. Using non-threatening questionnaires such as these can help break the ice, especially when difficult issues need to be addressed.

Finally, we hope you find this book a useful tool and enjoy supporting young people as much as we do! Hopefully we are all contributing to improving the lives of young people.

Confidential

Name _____ Form_____

What are your hobbies and interests?

_____

_____

What is your favourite...

Pop group? _____

Film? _____

Television programme? _____

Food? _____

Animal? _____

Day at school? _____

Lesson?_____

Who is your favourite teacher?

Who is your least favourite teacher?

What do you see yourself doing in ten years' time?

If you could do anything when you leave school, what would it be?

If you could change one thing about school, what would it be?

Thankyou!

What is Your Favourite...

TV programme?

Sweet?

Flim?

Animal?

Food?

Chapter One
EMOTIONAL INTELLIGENCE

Introduction

Someone who is emotionally intelligent can identify, express, understand and manage their emotions and can empathise with the emotions of others. Many of the difficulties encountered by young people in school might be attributable to a poor development of these skills. For example, anger management would be difficult to improve if the young person could not adequately identify and understand their emotions, making it a backbone to much of the work within this book. The order in which people improve these skills has been shown to be significant, as they need to be able to identify and name emotions before they can express them appropriately, and they need to be able to understand them before they will be able to control them. For further reading on this subject, see *Emotional Intelligence: Key Readings on the Mayer and Salovey Model* (Mayer and Salovey, 1997).

Primary schools have tackled this issue with the SEAL initiative (Social and Emotional Aspects of Learning), but secondary schools have not as widely adopted the secondary version, and perhaps the emphasis on achieving curriculum targets makes this less likely in any case. This makes the role of the mentor, being totally concerned with students' well-being, much more significant in filling the gap.

The exercises in this section cover all these different aspects of emotional intelligence, from mere recognition to empathy for others. There are a mixture of activities designed for use on a one-to-one basis, and those designed for group work, but many can be used for both. The key at the base of each sheet indicates which use is recommended.

One of the basic elements of this emotional intelligence section is a set of 90 Emotion Cards, which have been made as comprehensive as possible. These are designed to introduce new emotional vocabulary to young people, so they are better equipped to express exactly how they feel. The emoticon-style expressions are there to provide a visual clue to the word's meaning. We recommend that you photocopy them onto coloured card and, if possible, laminate them. This makes a very durable resource. Indeed, they can even be used in further chapters' activities.

Worksheets

What's in My Head?

This can be used in many ways, depending on the needs of the student, so has been deliberately kept non-directive. You could ask the student to write down his thoughts and feelings (using the Emotion

Cards if necessary). You could ask him to draw a series of symbols representing different thoughts and feelings, or you could ask him to draw one picture. Drawing can often help when the student is lost for words, and can be as abstract as he wishes. Recommended for individual use only.

Your Thoughts

This is a good introduction to looking at emotions, and helps students to start thinking and responding, as the questions are all concrete in nature.

Emotions

This sheet is rather more personal, and therefore carries a slightly higher risk factor than the previous worksheet. It may need to be completed with the Emotion Cards to choose from. It can be used in a one-off session, or re-visited several times to monitor progress.

How Do I Feel...

Some students feel happier drawing their responses rather than saying them. These worksheets cover basic emotions with a spare space for them to enter something more specific. It is good for younger students, and excellent for really quiet ones. It can be made into a small 'feelings' booklet if you staple the middle section. This will help those who find it difficult to talk about their emotions express them in a different way.

Word Association

This worksheet can be used on its own to look at how any chosen emotion looks, feels, acts, and so on. The emotion being considered is written in the centre shape. Responses to the questions can be drawn together into a multimedia collage-type picture of that emotion. This would work well in a group setting as a large wall picture depicting all the responses given by individual group members.

Individual Emotion Worksheets

These worksheets investigate specific emotions in more detail: sadness, love, hate, fear, hope, jealousy and loneliness. They can be used either with groups or individually as appropriate.

Activities

Emotion Cards

These cards can be used in any way you wish. All the suggestions are designed to improve young people's ability to identify, express, understand and control their emotions. The only limit is your own imagination! The following are some suggestions:

Ideas for use in one-to-one sessions
Sometimes students find it difficult to talk about their emotions. These cards are a great way to start even the quietest student talking.

- Ask the student to separate the cards into positive and negative emotions. Discuss with her what could cause each feeling.

- Sort through the cards first and remove those that are more complex. Ask the student to put the emotions in pairs of opposites. The student could then be asked to select which ones she feels most often. This will improve emotional vocabulary.

- Ask the student to sort the cards into groups of similar emotions. She could then be asked to choose one that she's experienced from each group. This improves emotional understanding.

- Ask the student to select from the pack all the emotions she has ever felt. Put aside the unselected ones. Working through the selected cards, ask the student to tell you about a specific time when she has felt each emotion. This aids identification of emotions.

- When addressing a specific incident, ask the student to select which emotions she felt at that time. Ask her to describe what that feeling felt like physically, and what thoughts were going through her head. This improves emotional understanding.

- Write scenarios about different situations (for example, bullying at school, confrontation at home, confrontation in the classroom, friendship difficulties) and ask the student to select two or three emotions that she imagines each character in the scenario feels. This can be developed to use with actual incidents, such as helping the student think how the teacher might feel in a confrontation that has recently taken place. This exercise helps to improve empathy skills.

Ideas for use in groups

- Emotions charades – split the group into two teams. Working through the cards (which have been previously sorted for appropriateness), one member from each team mimes the emotion. The student who guesses correctly collects that card for their team and then chooses the next card. The team with the most cards at the end wins. This helps young people to identify emotions in others, a key skill for empathy.

  Two variations on this theme could be to have the emotion expressed on paper (with no letters allowed) or to have it molded in modelling clay, with the other team guessing the emotion.

- Emotions sculpting – split the group into pairs. Each pair has an Emotions Card. One person 'sculpts' the other person into a shape expressing that emotion by manipulating their pose. It could be stated what the emotion is or left open for group members to guess. This improves emotional understanding and communication.

- Emotions bingo – the cards could be used to make a bingo game. Arrange them for a master copy in alphabetical order and photocopy. To make the game cards, choose at random 25 emotions for each (from the whole range each time) and photocopy these onto card in a five by five block. A good tip is to laminate the individual game cards, so that whiteboard pens can be used to mark 'called' emotions. These can then just be wiped at the end of the game ready for use again. The Emotion Cards can then be drawn at random by the caller and placed on the master copy, with the student marking their game card with a pen. This improves emotional vocabulary usage.

Pool of Emotions Game

This game takes place over stepping-stones around a pool of emotions. You will need a counter and two pass tokens for each player, some modelling clay, some extra paper and a pen, and a dice. It can be played by up to six people, including the mentor.

Preparation
The game layout should be pasted onto board for greater ease of play and durability. Photocopy one set of Emotion Cards and two sets of Action Cards. It is easier if the Emotion and Action Cards are different colours. Shuffle both sets of cards and put them on the appropriate spaces in the centre of the board.

To play
Each player takes it in turns to throw the dice and move the appropriate number of stepping-stones. If they stop on a green stepping stone, they have to take an Emotion Card (which they do not show

anyone) and an Action Card. The player has to follow the instructions on the action card, moving forward the appropriate number of stepping-stones if they are successful. If moving forwards takes them to another green stone, then they start their next turn with new Emotion and Action cards. Their used cards are then replaced at the bottom of the pack. Each player is equipped with two pass tokens, which they can use during the game if they are not prepared to complete the instruction on the action card. If they run out of tokens, any further refusal results in a missed turn. The winner is the first to reach the finish (an exact dice-throw is not needed!).

You may want to remove some of the action cards before the start of the game, depending on how emotionally intelligent the players are. Some of the tasks will carry too much risk for some students. Photocopy more of the cards chosen to make a bigger pile if some are removed. The omitted cards could be introduced as emotional intelligence increases.

Masks

Multimedia materials can be used to make a mask depicting a particular emotion (these could have a paper plate as a base or a cardboard cut-out shape). The emotion could be one that an individual is struggling with at the moment, or one that she would like to have. A mask could have two sides with opposite emotions on each side. For example, if the student feels sad and would like to feel happy, he could make a mask that is happy on one side and sad on the other. You could have a discussion afterwards about what steps he could take for him to move from sad to happy.

Song Emotions

This works well used with a group.

Choose a couple of contemporary songs that demonstrate contrasting emotions. Ask students to write down words about the emotions being expressed either on individual sheets to be pooled later, or on a central flipchart sheet using a marker pen.

Photo Emotions

Collect photos of people showing different emotions from magazines. Mount these individually on card to make them more durable. Ask the students (either individually or in a group) to choose a photo, and suggest two or three emotions that the person may be feeling. A development could be to devise a scenario as to why that person may be feeling those emotions. Alternatively, use the book *Reading Faces* (Maines, 2003), for a comprehensive set of 412 emotions photographs, and work with those.

Plasticine Emotions

This could be done either with selected Emotion Cards, an emotion the student is struggling with, or during work on a specific emotion in conjunction with the Individual Emotion worksheets. Give the student a lump of plasticine, and ask him to make a shape representing the emotion chosen. Explore what made him make the shape he chose.

Sayings for Life Game

There are many inspirational sayings being used in our schools nowadays, but how many do our young people actually understand? Lack of understanding would negate any application to their lives.

Many of these sayings use analogies and words with which young people are not familiar, and which they do not know how to interpret. They are commonly used in posters designed to inspire and motivate, and are displayed around schools, but the danger is that many young people will switch off if they do not understand the terminology that is used. This game encourages discussion and idea-pooling to gain insight and understanding. It is designed to inspire young people to think about a large range of sayings that they may or may not have encountered. After discussion, young people are much more likely to relate to these sayings. Due to the nature of the game, it would probably not be appropriate for young people with Asperger's syndrome, as they are often very literal thinkers, and would find the sayings difficult to understand.

Preparation
You will need a counter for each player and one dice.

To begin the game, you first need to make a game board. It is suggested that A1 is a good size of paper. The diagram below has been provided as a guide. You should draw a wobbly path of stepping-stones around the board from a spot marked 'start' to a spot marked 'finish'. About two thirds of these stepping-stones need to be yellow, and one third green (spread throughout the whole board). You will also need to copy the Category Cards and a set of the Sayings Cards (which would work well if they were laminated).

This game is for six players, including the facilitator. The complexity of some of the sayings means it is not designed to be played by students on their own, but rather with an adult who is able to adjudicate, offer prompts and hints, and encourage those who are not confident to take a guess.

The correct explanation or example of each saying acquires the young person something they need to succeed in life (be lenient in what you accept for explanation or example!). There are five categories that they need to collect: Friends, Food, Happiness, Fulfilment and Security.

To play
Shuffle the Category Cards so they are mixed together. Put them in a pile on the correct part of the board. Do the same with the Sayings Cards.

All players start on the start square.

Each player in turn throws the dice and moves the appropriate number of spaces. If he lands on a green square, he does not get the opportunity to take a Sayings Card and play moves round to the next player. If he lands on a yellow square, he takes a Sayings Card and reads it to the rest of the players. He then has to either offer a definition of the saying or an example of it in use. A correct answer gains him a chance to take the top card of the Category Cards pile.

Later on in the game, when some Category Cards have already been won, a player will pick up a card she already has. If this happens, then it is hard luck and she has to wait till her next turn to have another go!

Throwing a six ensures another go.

The person with all five of the category cards who lands on the finish square is the winner. If players land on the finish square without all the necessary Category Cards, then they have to go round the board again.

Helpful Contacts and Further Reading

http://nationalstrategies.standards.dcsf.gov.uk/primary/publications/banda/seal

Bar-On, R. and Parker, J. (2000) *The Handbook of Emotional Intelligence.* San Francisco: Jossey-Bass.

Goleman, D. (1995) *Emotional Intelligence: Why it Can Matter More Than IQ*. London: Bloomsbury.

Mayer, J. and Salovey, P. (1997) *What is Emotional Intelligence?* In Salovey, P., Brackett, M., and Mayer, J. (eds) *Emotional Intelligence: Key Readings on the Mayer and Salovey Model*. Port Chester, NY: National Professional Resources.

What's in My Head?

The Learning Mentor's Resource Book

Student use — Chapter One: Emotional Intelligence — 10-16

Photocopy or print from CD-ROM

Your Thoughts

1. What have you done that makes you most happy?

2. Do you like your name? Would you like to change it? What to?

3. What is the best thing that has ever happened to you?

4. What is the weirdest thing that has ever happened to you?

5. What is the silliest thing you have ever done?

6. What is the funniest thing that has ever happened to you?

7. Who do you admire and why?

8. What qualities do you look for in a friend?

9. What is the most important thing in your life?

10. What is your best quality?

11. What one thing would you change about yourself?

12. What one thing would you change about school?

13. What do you hate doing most in the world?

14. What do you like doing most in the world?

The Learning Mentor's Resource Book		
Student use	Chapter One: Emotional Intelligence	10-16
Photocopy or print from CD-ROM		

15

Emotions

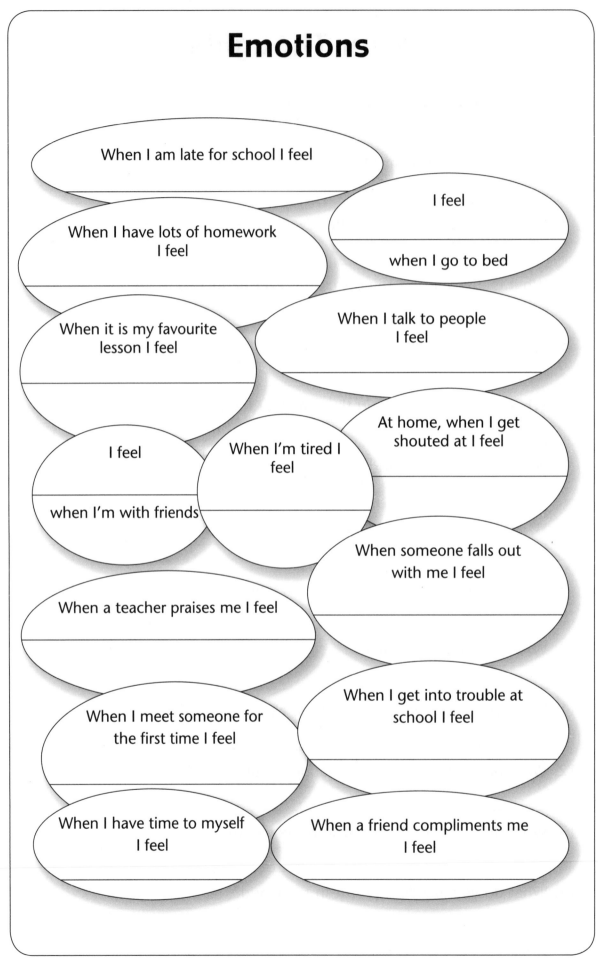

When I am late for school I feel

When I have lots of homework I feel

I feel _____ when I go to bed

When it is my favourite lesson I feel

When I talk to people I feel

I feel _____ when I'm with friends

When I'm tired I feel

At home, when I get shouted at I feel

When someone falls out with me I feel

When a teacher praises me I feel

When I get into trouble at school I feel

When I meet someone for the first time I feel

When I have time to myself I feel

When a friend compliments me I feel

The Learning Mentor's Resource Book

Student use | Chapter One: Emotional Intelligence

Photocopy or print from CD-ROM

11-16

How Do I Feel...

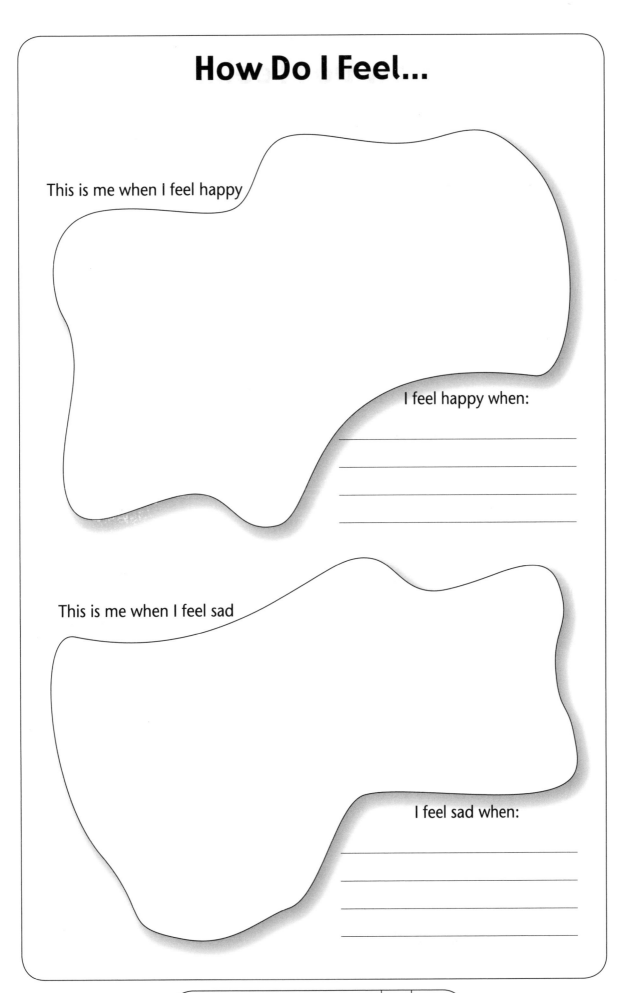

This is me when I feel happy

I feel happy when:

_____
_____
_____
_____

This is me when I feel sad

I feel sad when:

_____
_____
_____
_____

How Do I Feel...

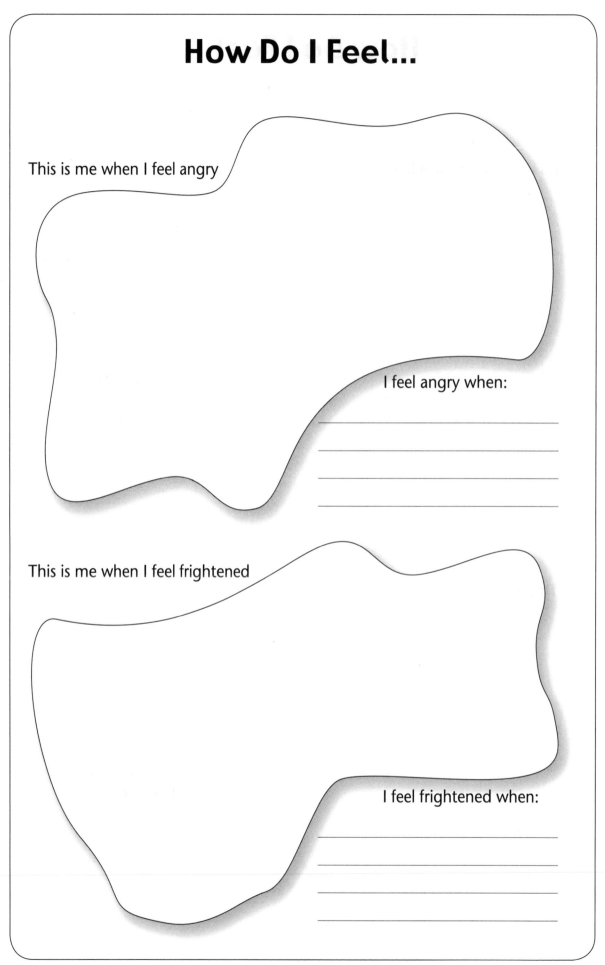

This is me when I feel angry

I feel angry when:

_____
_____
_____
_____

This is me when I feel frightened

I feel frightened when:

_____
_____
_____
_____

How Do I Feel...

This is me when I feel lonely

I feel lonely when:

_____

_____

_____

_____

This is me when I feel embarrassed

I feel embarrassed when:

_____

_____

_____

_____

How Do I Feel...

This is me when I am surprised

I am surprised when:

_____

_____

_____

_____

This is me when
I feel [   ]

I feel [   ]

when:

_____

_____

_____

The Learning Mentor's Resource Book

Student use | Chapter One: Emotional Intelligence

Photocopy or print from CD-ROM

10-14

Word Association

Texture...

_____

_____

Shape...

_____

_____

Sound...

_____

_____

_____

_____

Character...

_____

_____

Smell...

_____

_____

Animal...

_____

_____

Colour...

_____

_____

Individual Emotion Worksheet
Sadness

Which film makes you feel *sad?*

On a scale of 0–10, how often do
you feel sad? (0 means never and 10 means
all the time.)

Which song makes you feel *sad?*

0 1 2 3 4 5 6 7 8 9 10

What is your body's reaction when you feel sad?

Do you know what can make you feel better when you are sad?
If yes, write them down here. If not, you could ask someone else
to help you think of some ideas.

Here is a space to write down any other thoughts you might have.

_____

_____

_____

The Learning Mentor's Resource Book

Student use   Chapter One: Emotional Intelligence

Photocopy or print from CD-ROM

11-16

Individual Emotion Worksheet
Love

Name a food that you love:

Why do you love it?

Name a film that you love:

Why do you love it?

Name a place that you love:

Why do you love it?

Name a TV programme that you love:

Why do you love it?

Name a time of year that you love:

Why do you love it?

Name an animal that you love:

Why do you love it?

Name a song that you love:

Why do you love it?

Name a thing that you love:

Why do you love it?

Name a personal quality that you love:

Why do you love it?

Name a person that you love:

Why do you love them?

Individual Emotion Worksheet
Hate

Colour in the boxes to show how much you hate the things below!

10 means you really hate it

1 means you don't hate it at all

Add some ideas of your own...

	1	2	3	4	5	6	7	8	9	10
School										
Vegetables										
Homework										
Cold weather										
Getting up										
Bullies										
The dentist										

The Learning Mentor's Resource Book
Student use   Chapter One: Emotional Intelligence
Photocopy or print from CD-ROM

11-16

Individual Emotion Worksheet
I Fear...

1. One animal I would not like to meet face to face is

_____

2. One person I fear is

_____

3. One experience I fear is

_____

4. One film that made me feel fear was

_____

5. One fear I would like to conquer is

_____

6. One fear I have conquered is

_____

7. One fear in other people that I find hard to understand is

_____

Individual Emotion Worksheet
Fear

How much do you fear…

Mark on the 1–5 scale how much you fear the thought of the following things, with 5 being frightened stiff and 1 being cool as a cucumber!

1. Riding on a really fast high rollercoaster (1) (2) (3) (4) (5)

2. Going to the dentist (1) (2) (3) (4) (5)

3. Spiders (1) (2) (3) (4) (5)

4. Snakes (1) (2) (3) (4) (5)

5. Getting things wrong (1) (2) (3) (4) (5)

6. Heights (1) (2) (3) (4) (5)

7. Rock-climbing up a mountain (1) (2) (3) (4) (5)

8. Scuba diving (1) (2) (3) (4) (5)

9. Wasps (1) (2) (3) (4) (5)

10. Dogs (1) (2) (3) (4) (5)

11. Watching a really scary film (1) (2) (3) (4) (5)

12. Failure (1) (2) (3) (4) (5)

13. Potholing (1) (2) (3) (4) (5)

14. Exams (1) (2) (3) (4) (5)

15. Singing in front of an audience on your own (1) (2) (3) (4) (5)

Individual Emotion Worksheet
Hope

Describe what hope is…

I hope I will always…

_____

I hope I will work as…

_____

I hope that when I leave school…

_____

I hope I can improve…

_____

I hope I won't…

_____

I hope my future…

_____

I hope I will become…

_____

Individual Emotion Worksheet
Jealousy

What makes you jealous?

Tick all the situations that would make you feel jealous.

Then pick your top three.

☐ Your friend has a brand new games console that makes yours seem ancient.

☐ Your brother is bought an ice cream and you are not.

☐ Your friend gets better marks in a maths test than you.

☐ Your friend wins a prize puzzle competition.

☐ Your boy/girlfriend tells you how they met one of your mates in town and went for a burger.

☐ Your mum has a brand new baby and doesn't have time to help you with homework or even sign your planner.

☐ You are dumped by your boy/girlfriend and they end up going out with your cousin.

☐ Your dad's new wife has had a baby and he tells you that you won't be able to come and stay for a while.

☐ Your older brother has just got his GCSE results and you know you cannot do as well.

☐ You spot your boy/girlfriend fl irting with someone else at a party.

☐ Your mate decides to hang about with someone else who you don't get on with.

The Learning Mentor's Resource Book
Student use | Chapter One: Emotional Intelligence
Photocopy or print from CD-ROM
11-16

Individual Emotion Worksheet
Loneliness

You have been stranded on a desert island.

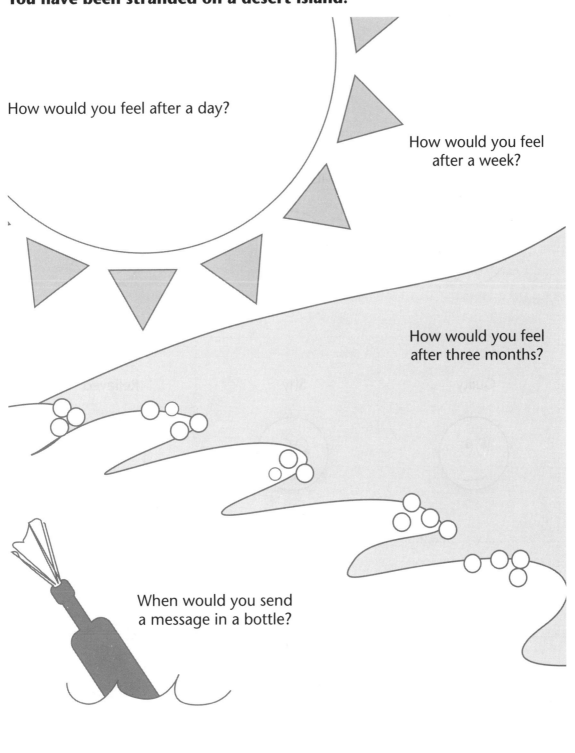

How would you feel after a day?

How would you feel after a week?

How would you feel after three months?

When would you send a message in a bottle?

Emotion Cards

Surprised	Miserable	Depressed
Hurt	Mischievous	Peaceful
Guilty	Shy	Relieved
Sure	Regretful	Satisfied

The Learning Mentor's Resource Book

Student use   Chapter One: Emotional Intelligence

Photocopy or print from CD-ROM

10-16

Emotion Cards

Curious	Apathetic	Helpless
Puzzled	Envious	Anxious
Undecided	Frightened	Cautious
Sorry	Lonely	Paranoid

Emotion Cards

Thoughtful	Disgusted	Confident
Loved	Innocent	Withdrawn
Hopeful	Generous	Brave
Giggly	Grateful	Glad

The Learning Mentor's Resource Book
Student use | Chapter One: Emotional Intelligence
Photocopy or print from CD-ROM
10-16

Emotion Cards

Friendly	Relaxed	Different
Flippant	Secretive	Sneaky
Grumpy	Gloomy	Yucky
Worried	Lost	Naughty

Emotion Cards

Unsettled	Misunderstood	Mad
Awful	Ashamed	Abandoned
Violent	Pained	Suspicious
Shocked	Enthusiastic	Embarrassed

The Learning Mentor's Resource Book

Student use   Chapter One: Emotional Intelligence

Photocopy or print from CD-ROM

10-16

Emotion Cards

Confused	Bored	Angry
Disappointed	Interested	Excited
Sad	Aggressive	Exhausted
Happy	Alienated	Hostile

Emotion Cards

Annoyed	Scared	Proud
Negative	Stubborn	Determined
Frustrated	Discouraged	Delighted
Pleased	Amused	Controlled

The Learning Mentor's Resource Book

Student use | Chapter One: Emotional Intelligence

Photocopy or print from CD-ROM

10-16

Pool of Emotions Game

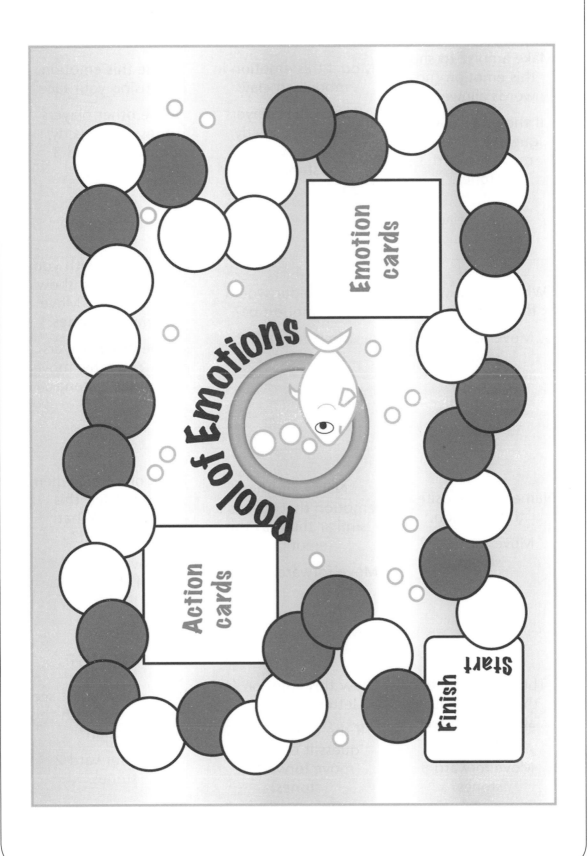

Pool of Emotions: Action Cards

Make a noise to show this emotion (no words allowed!). If the other players guess it correctly, move forward 3 stones.	Model this emotion in modelling clay. If the other players guess it correctly, move forward 3 stones.	Mime this emotion only using your face. If the other players guess it correctly, move forward 3 stones.
What animal would this emotion be? Move forward 2 stones.	What colour would this emotion be? Move forward 2 stones.	Strike a pose with your whole body to show this emotion. Move forward 2 stones. If the other players guess correctly, move a further 2 stones.
Name the opposite of this emotion. Move forward 2 stones.	Name another emotion that means a similar thing as this emotion. Move forward 1 stone.	Think of a time when you last felt this emotion. What happened? Move forward 4 stones.
Think of a situation that would cause someone to feel like this. Move forward 3 stones.	Draw this emotion (no letters allowed!). If the other players guess it correctly, move forward 3 stones.	When did you last see someone else with this emotion? Move forward 2 stones.

Sayings for Life!

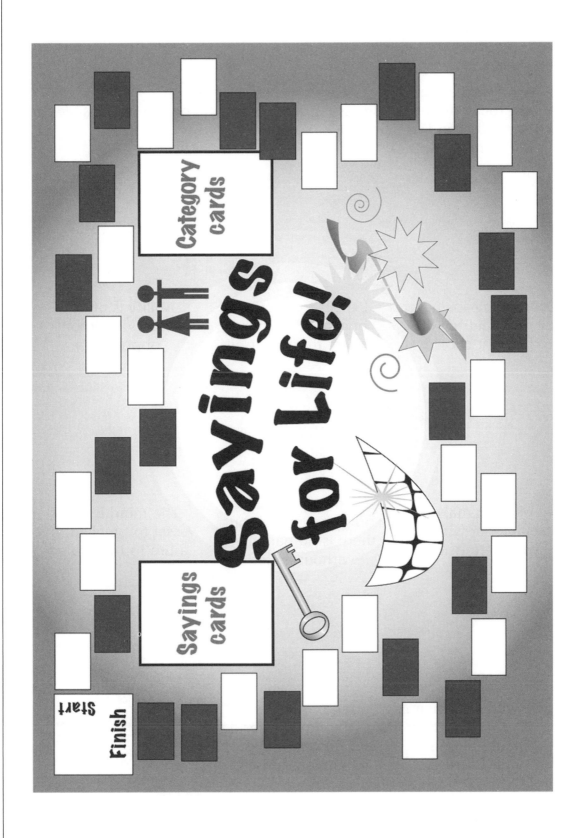

Sayings Cards

Let the choices you make today be the choices you can live with tomorrow.	Be responsible. Actions have consequences.	You are responsible for you.
Courage means never being afraid to voice the right choice.	Expect from others only what you first expect from yourself.	Ability is of little account without opportunity.
No one can make you feel inferior without your permission.	Action may not always bring happiness, but there is no happiness without action.	The mind is not a vessel to be filled, but a fire to be kindled.
Voice without action is a daydream. Action without vision is a nightmare.	Everyone thinks of changing the world, but no one thinks of changing himself.	Real knowledge is to know the extent of one's ignorance.

Sayings Cards

Excellence knows no gender.	Today is your chance to make a difference. What are you waiting for?	Your never know how much you can do till you try.
You may never know the answer if you don't ask the question.	Imagine venturing beyond the obvious to discover what others don't see.	Imagine life as more than a spectator sport.
Diversity creates dimension in our world.	Your choices. Your actions. Your life.	Doing what is right isn't always easy, but it's always right.
For success, attitude is as important as ability.	The choices we don't make are as important as the ones we do make.	We are all one race – human.

Sayings Cards

The highest fences we need to climb are those we've built within our minds.	Life is full of choices – choose carefully.	We can only see with open eyes; we can only hear with open ears; we can only think with open minds.
Self-control is knowing you can, but deciding you won't.	Say what you mean, mean what you say.	Telling a lie is like seeing a ghost – it can come back to haunt you.
Respect is not a gift – you have to earn it.	Stand up for what is right, even if you're standing alone.	Respect yourself. If you don't nobody will.
You are as honest as your actions.	Courage is doing right when everyone around you is doing wrong.	Who you are begins with what you do.

Sayings Cards

Be somebody you would be proud to know.	If you expect respect, be the first to show it.	Respect – you gotta give it to get it.
Aspire to climb as high as you can dream.	Always set the trail, never follow the path.	Most people are about as happy as they make up their minds to be.
Believe in yourself – dare to dream.	To get started, you must have a destination.	Today's preparation determines tomorrow's achievement.
Great opportunities are often disguised as unsolvable problems.	Excellence = motivation × confidence.	Anger can severely limit your choices.

Sayings Cards

The most important decision in your life is to like and accept yourself.	Change your thinking to change your feelings.	Do what you can with what you have where you are.
Only you can change your attitude.	You can't aim too high.	An error doesn't become a mistake until you refuse to correct it.
Self-improvement starts with self-control.	What is popular is not always right, what is right is not always popular.	A man's true wealth is the good he does in the world.
Consider those whom you call your enemies and figure our what they should call you.	Anyone who has never made a mistake has never done anything new.	As you sow, so you reap.

Sayings Cards

All progress has resulted from people who took unpopular decisions.	Injustice anywhere is a threat to justice everywhere.	In the middle of difficulty lies opportunity.
Life is a tennis game. You can't win without serving.	Success doesn't come to you – you go to it.	The art of being wise is the art of knowing what to overlook.
The journey of a thousand miles begins with a single step.	To see what is right and not to do it is to lack courage.	Build bridges not barriers.
Fight the problem not the person.	Conflict comes, not from our differences, but from how we manage those differences.	Start from the point of agreement rather than disagreement.

Sayings Cards

No one can do everything but everyone can do something.	No act of kindness, no matter how small, was ever wasted.	Attitude is the mind's paintbrush. It can colour any situation.
The most important thing about goals is having one.	In order to win you must expect to win.	All things are difficult before they are easy.

The Learning Mentor's Resource Book
Student use   Chapter One: Emotional Intelligence
Photocopy or print from CD-ROM

12-16

Category Cards: Friends

Category Cards: Food

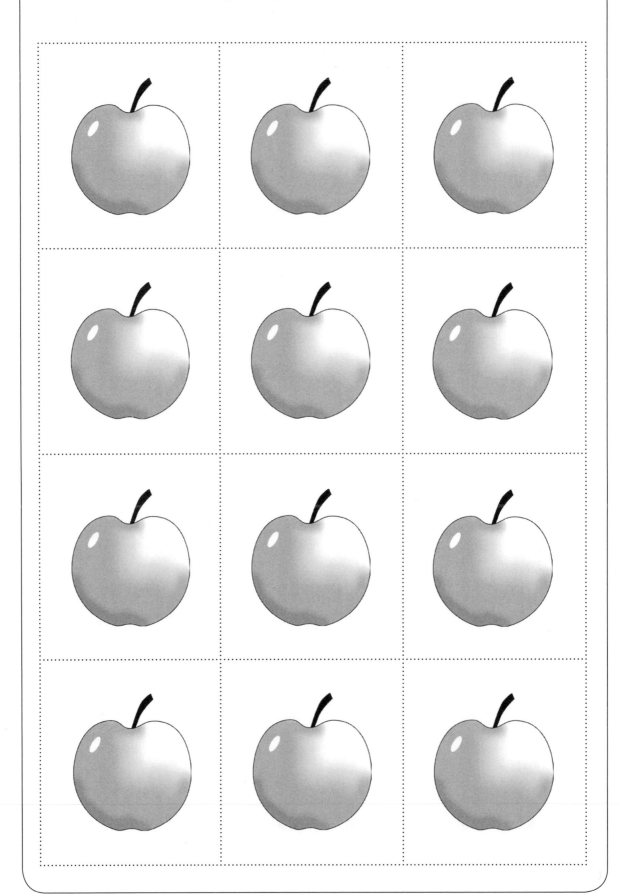

The Learning Mentor's Resource Book

Student use | Chapter One: Emotional Intelligence

Photocopy or print from CD-ROM

12-16

Category Cards: Happiness

Category Cards: Fulfilment

Category Cards: Security

The Learning Mentor's Resource Book		
Student use	Chapter One: Emotional Intelligence	12-16
Photocopy or print from CD-ROM		

51

Chapter Two
SELF-ESTEEM

Introduction

Most research identifies low self-esteem as a contributing factor in much of the disaffection we see in young people. The origins of this trend could stem from a variety of sources, such as family, traumatic experiences, bullying, peer pressure to conform to a certain image and media pressure to look a certain way. There are many, often combined, messages given to young people implying that they are just not good enough.

Self-esteem is the way we view ourselves, compared to our ideal self. If, in a student's own mind, she falls short of how attractive, clever or loved she thinks she should be, then this will have a negative impact on her self-esteem in these areas. It could be that a student's self-esteem is high academically, but low physically. Students are known to reject praise for their achievements, or even destroy the work that earned the praise in the first place, because their low self-esteem in this area means that any praise is contrary to their own view of themselves and thus the student may feel their world-view is threatened. It is safer to stick with the uncomfortable known than the risky unknown. Alternatively, she may not be used to receiving praise. This makes self-esteem quite a tricky area to work with, as there is often natural resistance to the student changing her own view of herself, due to the vulnerable position that puts her in.

The worksheets in this section mostly take a cognitive-behavioural approach and start by assessing self-esteem before narrowing down the particularly vulnerable areas. They then move on to self-awareness, so that the student can become acquainted with the reality of who she is, and they end with some worksheets designed specifically to raise self-esteem.

A word of caution is raised at this point for the more problematic examples of a student whose self-esteem is low across the board (although this is rare) or when it results from more entrenched family issues. If a child's parent has been unavailable in their early years, through depression, mental health issues, their own life difficulties or substance misuse, this often results in the young person feeling unsafe within herself and thus lacking in self-esteem. Good self-esteem is a resilience factor and is strongly linked with family experiences and positive attachment. Furthermore, for families where parents themselves have not had a positive experience of being parented or who are struggling with busy lifestyles it can be difficult to spend time with their children, give praise or maintain boundaries. Without this positive attention and guidance, issues with self-esteem can develop and present in the form of poor confidence, low mood or behavioural problems. It may be more useful in such cases to support the parents in joining a parent support programme, a number of which are now being delivered by local councils, health and education services. Children and young people respond most to positive attention from their parents so without this, one-to-one work on self-esteem may not have any significant effect.

Worksheets

My Self-image

This worksheet is a great way of finding out which areas are particularly sensitive for students and also for measuring improvements in self-esteem. The student chooses a coloured pen and makes a mark in the first box 'Where I am now' at the bottom of the sheet. He then reads both sections on the sheet, putting a mark where he feels he is now in terms of self-esteem in all the areas listed. 0 means he does not think he is like this and 5 means he is a lot like this. After that, he selects another colour, marks the other box, 'Where I would like to be' at the bottom of the page and reads through all the areas again, this time marking where he would like to be. After that has been done, the difference between the two colours needs to be added up (by counting how many black lines are between each mark, for example, if he has put the first mark for 'happy' on 2 and the second mark for it on 5, than the difference would be 3).

If the student has a large difference between his perceived position now and his ideal position, a low self-esteem in that area is indicated. The totals for each line can be added up and then compared to a re-working of the same sheet after some self-esteem work has been done. If the number for each category is less, this indicates that self-esteem has improved.

Self-esteem Factors

The purpose of this is for the student to think of the different factors that contribute to positive self esteem and those that can damage it, without making it a personal question. It can be done in a general sense if she is not yet ready to face areas of her life that are difficult. The sheet can be re-visited later to see how many of the factors she listed she can personally relate to, and whether any others have come to light during the course of the work.

Me and My Body

This is perhaps more relevant to girls than boys, but not exclusively. It gives permission for the student to actually say what she doesn't like and would change if she could, but it also moves her forward to a point of questioning where she is getting that aspiration from.

If I Were…

This calls for some imagination and can cause some hilarity! It is essentially a light-hearted way of encouraging a student to look at himself and what defines him. Although it looks like a bit of fun, some serious points can arise. This can really illuminate how he sees himself.

Pen Portraits

This worksheet asks the student to compose a pen portrait about a person that the student admires.

There are two questions in the first section of the pen portrait, which will hopefully add some structure to the way he thinks about what to write. These questions are intended to apply to all three sections. You should respond to what has been written in each section, drawing similarities between the student and his role model.

You could also investigate why the student finds these characteristics important.

Likes and Dislikes

This worksheet allows the student to think what it is about himself that he doesn't like but also requires him to think of some positive things as well. Some of the negative things could be realistic difficulties, but they could also only be the student's own perception, so the student may need challenging as to where he got the idea that he is a certain way from.

Other People

This is useful if a student is having difficulty with peer relationships. It could help to analyse where the difficulties are and shape future work. It could also show inconsistencies in how much other people like her, compared to how much she likes herself. This may be useful in planting seeds of doubt about how accurate her own view of herself is.

Things I Enjoy Doing/ My Happy Memories/ My Good Points

These worksheets are all looking at only positive things. Sometimes thinking can become so negative that the student actually finds it very difficult to think of positive points. These sheets may need to be filled in and added to over time, as work continues, as the student may find filling in all the spaces too difficult to begin with. They can be used again as new strengths and interests are discovered.

Changing Ourselves

Sometimes young people can only see change on a macro scale and find it difficult to break down bigger difficulties into smaller tasks. This is one way of encouraging the student to think small! She will feel encouraged if some of these tiny steps are achieved and will be more able to see change as something that is achievable, rather than impossible.

This sheet may also be useful used in conjunction with the sheets in the Self-harm and Behaviour Change chapters (Chapter Five and Chapter Ten).

Ten Good Things About Me

This really moves the student towards thinking about the positive aspects that he has about his character. It may need to be added to over time and a task can be set to think of a couple of new positive aspects to add each week.

I am Unique – Special

This is a way to help a student recognise that she is special, whatever other circumstances seem to suggest. Have an ink stamp pad ready and ask the student to put her fingerprints in the box. She can take the piece of paper home to remind her that she really is unique!

I am Proud That...

Being proud is often looked upon as arrogance, but students need to develop the skill of being able to be proud when the situation warrants it. This sheet develops the sense of pride by recording achievements and personal qualities. The message is that it is OK to feel proud of oneself and we all have reasons to feel proud.

Thought Changing

We all, to some extent, have a voice in our heads telling us that we are no good, or that we cannot do something. This helps a student to identify that this negative thought process is actually happening and to change those negatives to positives.

In the explosion shape, the student writes a negative thought that he consistently experiences. Then in the oval shape, help him to change that negative thought into a positive one. For example, 'I find it difficult to make friends. I never have any friends anyway, so there's no point in trying.' Change that thought to: 'I find it difficult to make friends, but if I am really friendly and start by just smiling, then someone may decide to talk to me.' Begin with the reality of the situation, but then change to a more positive outcome.

Positive Thinking

This is a diary-type of exercise to encourage a lifestyle of positive thinking. The student takes the sheet away and has to think of at least one positive thought each day and write this down. After a week, she can bring the sheet back and you can reflect together on the positive nature of the week.

Receiving Compliments

Receiving compliments is a remarkably difficult thing to do and something that we are generally not very good at. The sad fact is that we are not used to receiving compliments, as statistics show that by the time we are eighteen years old we will have received 250,000 negative comments and only 25,000 positive ones, most of which were said before the age of three. This sheet explores some of the thoughts and feelings behind receiving compliments.

An interesting way to start the exercise is to think of a genuine compliment to pay the student and then explore how it made him feel. You could also progress a step further by posing the question, 'When did you last give someone a compliment?' This can lead on to a discussion about how little this happens in our society.

Activities

Lifeline

Give the student a large (A3) piece of paper or card to work on and some felt tip pens. Ask her to mark a point near the top left-hand corner 'birth', and a point near the bottom right-hand corner 'death'. Ask her then to fix a point in the middle of the sheet and mark it 'Me Now'. The student has to then connect the points in a lifeline of events that have already happened (birth to now), and events she would like to happen (between now and death). She can do this in any way she would like. It could be a simple wavy line snaking across the page with pictures and words coming off it, or it could be a series of stepping-stones with illustrations and captions within them. Encourage her to be as creative and artistic as she likes.

Some questions could be asked after she has completed the lifeline. For example: 'Is there anything that surprised you?', 'Is there something you would change?', 'Is there something you have to achieve to get the future you would like?' Be led by the way she has done the lifeline, encouraging explanation of unexpected elements.

Sensitivity warning: think about the student's background when deciding to use this exercise; there may be modifications you would like to make to render it more suitable.

Inside/Outside Self

Using a box of plastic animals, or shells, or stones – something with some variety – ask the student to choose one to represent the way he is outside to the rest of the world. Ask him to choose another stone that represents how he feels on the inside. Talk through the differences and what has caused them.

Another way to do this is to have some collage and craft materials available, and a piece of A4 card, the task being to make a double-sided mask of those two different aspects of his personality. If those types of materials are not available, then you could use pictures and ask him to draw himself outside and inside.

Personal Collage

Using an A3 sheet of card or paper, the student covers it in images from magazines (and own photographs, if she has been warned beforehand) that represent some positive aspect of herself. Words from magazines and newspapers can be useful as well. Ask her to present the personal collage to you, explaining all the images and why they are relevant.

You could also use the SWOT Analysis and Personal Crest sheets from the behaviour section of this book (Chapter Ten).

Pay Yourself Some Compliments

Have some fluorescent stars (about 5 centimetres wide) ready and ask the student to write a compliment to herself on each one. You can suggest finishing the sentence: 'I am a star because...' She should then stick as many as she can think of (and if she cannot think of any, start with a genuine compliment from you) onto a sheet of A4 card entitled: 'I am a star because...'

Helpful Contacts and Further Reading

www.selfesteembooksforchildren.com

www.selfesteem2go.com

Holland, S. and Ward, C. (2002) *Assertiveness: A Practical Approach*. Oxon: Speechmark Publishing.

Plummer, D. (2007) *Helping Children to Build Self-Esteem: A Photocopiable Activities Book*, second edition. London: Jessica Kingsley Publishers.

My Self-image

0 means not at all   5 means very much

Area	0	1	2	3	4	5
Happy						
Kind						
Friendly						
Helpful						
Clever						
Popular						
Good sense of humour						
Considerate						
Good looking						
Sporty						
Hard working						
Lucky						

Area	0	1	2	3	4	5
Jealous						
Bullying						
Easily bored						
Annoying						
Lonely						
Bad tempered						
Silly						
Moody						
Shy						
Cheeky						
Bossy						
Easily worried						

☐ Where I am now
☐ Where I would like to be

The Learning Mentor's Resource Book

Student use | Chapter Two: Self-esteem

Photocopy or print from CD-ROM

11-16

Self-esteem Factors

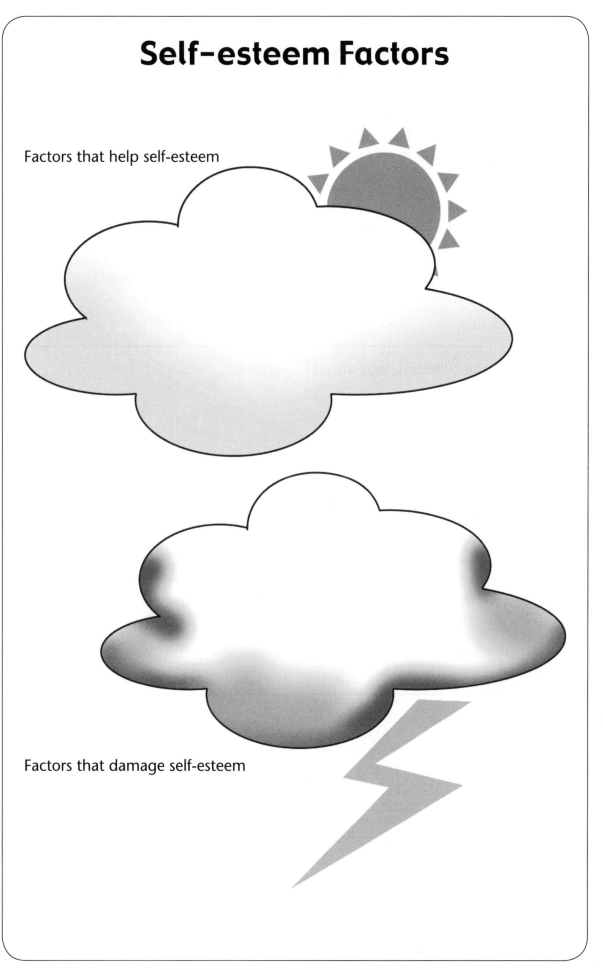

Factors that help self-esteem

Factors that damage self-esteem

Me and My Body

What do you think of your body?
What influences the way you see yourself?
What are you self-conscious about?
Do you want to change your body?
If you were to change your body, what would you do?
Who are your role models?
Do you feel pressurised into looking like them?

The Learning Mentor's Resource Book

Student use | Chapter Two: Self-esteem

Photocopy or print from CD-ROM

10-16

If I Were...

If I were an animal I would be a...

If I were a car I would be a...

If I were a TV programme I would be...

If I were a building I would be a...

If I were a sport I would be...

If I were a food I would be...

If I were a game I would be a...

If I were a plant I would be a...

Pen Portraits

	1. What makes them tick?	2. What delights/ motivates/scares them?
Write a pen portrait of someone you admire…		
Write a pen portrait about your best friend…		
Write a pen portrait about yourself…		

Likes and Dislikes

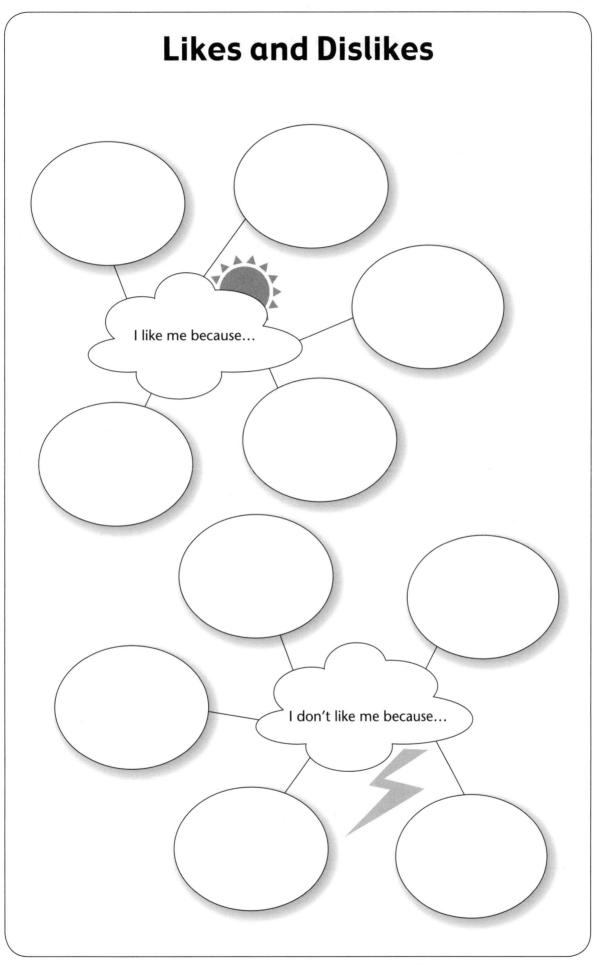

I like me because…

I don't like me because…

The Learning Mentor's Resource Book		
Student use	Chapter Two: Self-esteem	10-16
Photocopy or print from CD-ROM		

61

Other People

Other people like me because...	Other people don't like me because...

I like me because...	I don't like me because...

The Learning Mentor's Resource Book

Student use   Chapter Two: Self-esteem

Photocopy or print from CD-ROM

10-16

Things I Enjoy Doing

The Learning Mentor's Resource Book		
Student use	Chapter Two: Self-esteem	10-16
Photocopy or print from CD-ROM		

63

My Happy Memories

My Good Points

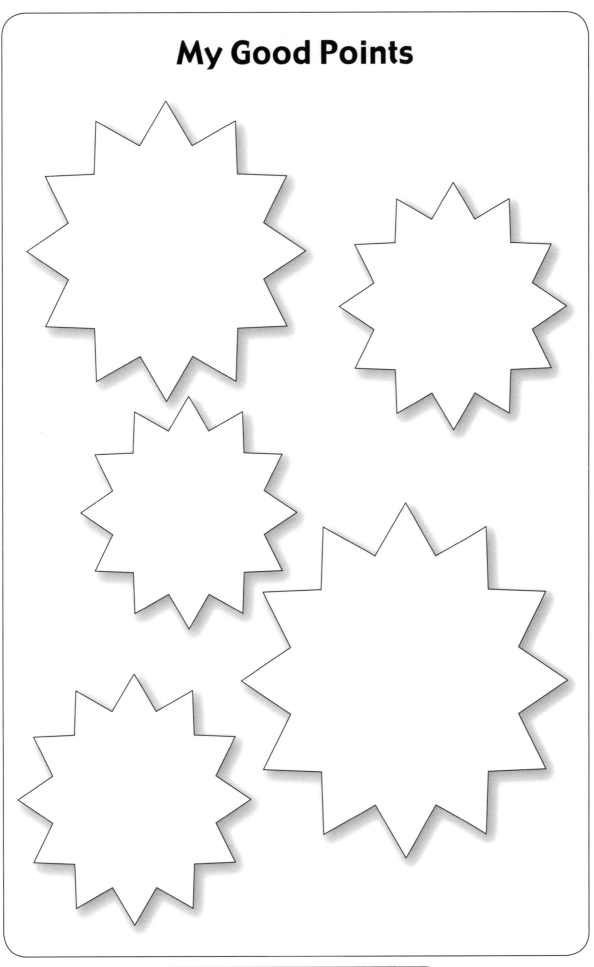

Changing Ourselves

It has been said that to change something 100%, it is only necessary to change 100 things by 1%.

List ten tiny changes you would like to make in your life...

1. _____

_____

2. _____

_____

3. _____

_____

4. _____

_____

5. _____

_____

6. _____

_____

7. _____

_____

8. _____

_____

9. _____

_____

10. _____

_____

The Learning Mentor's Resource Book

Student use | Chapter Two: Self-esteem

Photocopy or print from CD-ROM

10-16

Ten Good Things About Me

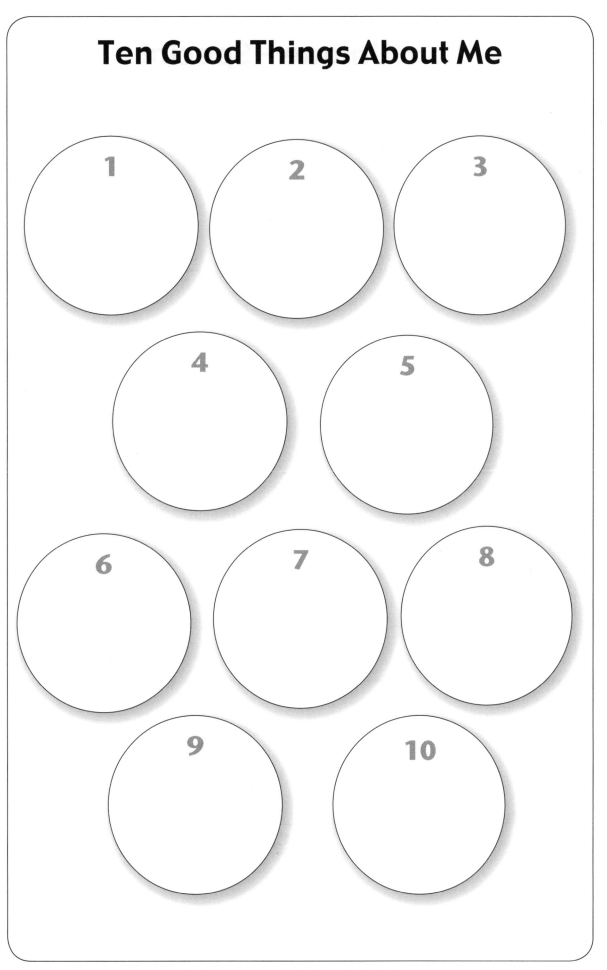

The Learning Mentor's Resource Book		
Student use	Chapter Two: Self-esteem	10-16
Photocopy or print from CD-ROM		

67

I am Unique – Special

There is no one else like me!

The Learning Mentor's Resource Book		
Student use	Chapter Two: Self-esteem	10-16
Photocopy or print from CD-ROM		

I am Proud That...

I am proud that...

1. My family is

[   ]

2. I tried hard to

[   ]

3. I did well in

[   ]

4. I am good at

[   ]

5. I did not

[   ]

6. I helped

[   ]

7. I always

[   ]

8. I have improved at

[   ]

9. I will become

[   ]

10. My ambition is to

[   ]

The Learning Mentor's Resource Book
Student use | Chapter Two: Self-esteem
Photocopy or print from CD-ROM
10-16

69

Thought Changing

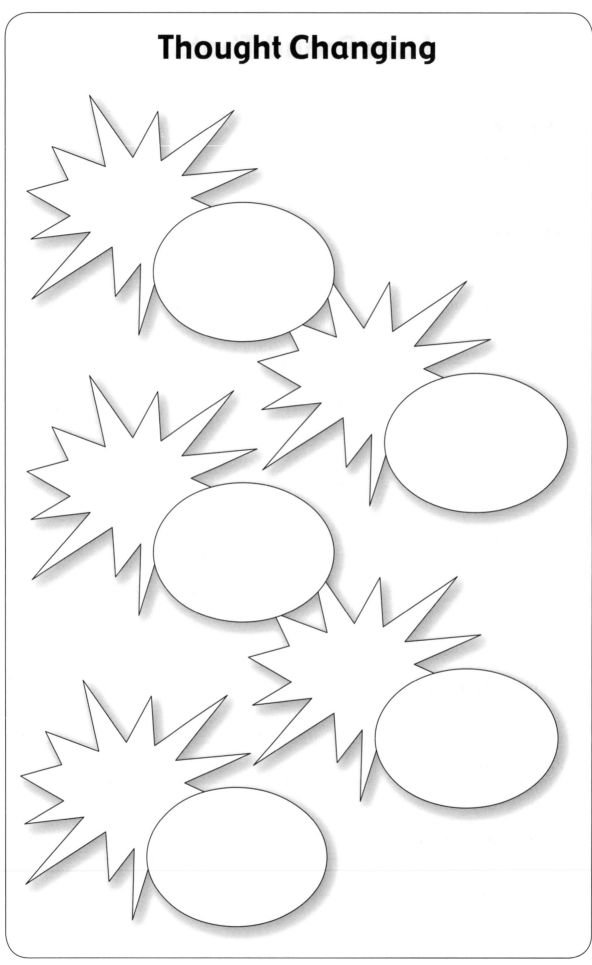

Positive Thinking

Monday

_____

_____

Tuesday

_____

_____

Wednesday

_____

_____

Thursday

_____

_____

Friday

_____

_____

Saturday

_____

_____

Sunday

_____

_____

Receiving Compliments

What are the good things about receiving compliments?

What are the difficult things about receiving compliments?

Chapter Three
ANGER MANAGEMENT

Introduction

Learning to control anger is a skill that we all need. Students encountering difficulties in school often find that this is an area in which they feel they have little or no control, causing them to 'explode' when someone stumbles upon one of their triggers. Often this is not something either person is aware of, making for a reaction no one really understands. Young people will have little control over their triggers, but building an awareness of what they are can help to improve their reactions. The learning mentor can inform staff of certain trigger areas to avoid once they are discovered in a student who often displays angry outbursts in the classroom. Often peers who discover someone's trigger will provoke that person deliberately because it will invariably create a show for them to sit back and watch!

The anger management worksheets follow a pattern, introducing anger as being similar to a bomb. The triggers light the fuse and the bomb explodes after the flame reaches it. This 'fuse' time can be incredibly short and if control is to be maintained, work must be done to lengthen it. Once the bomb has exploded, the student is no longer capable of rational thought.

Worksheets

Beware: Anger Bomb!

This sheet is designed as a visual aid for use with the student to demonstrate how anger works, as part of the problem is a lack of understanding. This reinforces, in concrete terms, that even the weakest student can gain some understanding.

Explain that when they have an angry outburst, their anger bomb has exploded. Take the process back to the first action required, that of lighting the fuse. Explain that everyone has triggers which cause their fuse to be lit, and the first job is to find out exactly what they are. Then go on to explain that the longer the fuse is, the more likely they are to be able to do something to stop it reaching the bomb. The activities that follow are then centred on lengthening the fuse and damping down the flame.

Anger Pie

This exercise helps the student to discover in which areas he becomes most angry. Following the instructions on the sheet, he should end up with an appropriately coloured pie chart. Hopefully one or two areas will have significantly more colour on them than the others. These are the areas in which he has most difficulty. You could then explore what it is about these areas that provoke his anger, asking the student to write key words in that slice of pie.

What Makes You Angry?

This is a more specific exploration of a student's triggers. Follow the instructions on the worksheet. The student can fill in her own more specific triggers in the blank section. Relate the areas ticked to the bomb picture, explaining that these are the things that light her fuse. At the end of the exercise you should have three triggers that are the most significant for that particular student. These can then be explored with the following worksheet.

Thoughts – Feelings – Actions

It is not usually the trigger itself that causes anger but the student's own thoughts about that trigger. Deciding that something was done deliberately rather than accidentally is more likely to make the reaction an angry one. Using the key three triggers that were identified with the previous worksheet, this worksheet can either investigate them all together or be used three times to cover them more individually. The student needs to explore what her thoughts towards the triggers are, what feelings are experienced (the Emotion Cards are a useful resource to use here), and what these feelings cause her to do in her anger. This approach linking thoughts to feelings and actions is an important strand of Cognitive Behavioural Therapy.

Lengthening the Fuse

Relate this to the bomb picture again and explain that to actually change the way triggers are thought about can change the reaction, and so lengthen the fuse. For example, if a student always becomes angry when someone calls his family names, then he is getting angry because he thinks that person knows something about his family, is passing judgement, that this is what is really thought and that everyone else will believe it too. In reality this name-calling is often done by students who know nothing about another student's family but use it merely as a way to wind him up. The name caller doesn't believe what she is saying because she knows that she has made it up, and so does everyone else. If the student can recognise these facts, then he is less likely to explode. The realisation that someone is only saying it because they get such a wonderful reaction can be very powerful. Similarly, the student who is pushed in the corridor can decide whether to think it was deliberate or an accident. That decision will shape that student's response.

It takes practice to change thinking patterns, but working through different scenarios can help. In this worksheet, three major triggers can be written in the first shape, and alternative more helpful thoughts written in the connecting shape.

Putting Out the Flame

This page is designed to be photocopied onto card and cut up into individual reference cards.

The cards are self-explanatory, but the key is that they must be practised to be of any use in a situation of high anger arousal. Work through them with the student. With younger students, it may be advisable to give them one a week to practise and report back on. Some role-play is also useful. Parents or carers can be asked to assist, if appropriate.

When cards of most use are selected, they can be fixed together into a reference pack with a hole-punch and short treasury tag. Keep the instruction card at the front of the pack (the card at the top left hand corner of the sheet). The student then has prompts to remind her how to act when she begins to feel angry.

Physical Anger

This worksheet helps students to recognise when they are becoming angry, so they know they need to start using some of the fuse-lengthening strategies outlined earlier. Relate this to the bomb picture, so they can see that this is how they feel when someone has just lit their fuse.

Using the body outline, students mark what physical changes happen when they start to feel angry. These might include reactions such as a thumping heart, sweaty palms, hot face, shaking legs and so on.

Time-out Cards

With some students given to loud and alarming explosions of anger, some schools will allow them to have a time-out facility. This means that such students are issued with 'Time-out Cards' which can be given to their teacher when they feel angry. The example below is to show what the card could look like and can be altered for relevance to other situations. Use a deliberately calm colour (such as green) rather than the more inflammatory red.

```
-----------------------------------------------------------------

     Learning Mentor Green Card

         Please let me leave the lesson to see my learning mentor.

                         Thank you.

-----------------------------------------------------------------
```

We would recommend laminating this card for more durability and also writing the student's name on the back indelibly so that it does not become currency for any student to remove themselves from a lesson. It needs to be carefully explained to the student that the card must be used as soon as she feels the physical anger signs starting because if she waits until the bomb has exploded, rational thought has gone and unfortunate things can be said and done.

If a student arrives in a state of anger to you, having used her card, it is essential that she is allowed some time to calm herself down before anyone attempts to quiz her about the incident.

Anger Line

This worksheet can be used as a resource at this point, for her to complete entirely on her own. We would also recommend that another calming activity be given to her, such as colouring, using modeling clay or drawing. Many students already know some things that they can do to calm themselves down. On the issue of a Time-out Card, try to ascertain what these might be, and have the appropriate materials on hand to use.

Activities

Anger Collage

The student is given a blank piece of white A3 paper and some glue, collage materials and colours. Allow him to create a picture of what his anger feels like. You may have to go through some of his individual anger situations in order to help him feel what it is like. This activity can also be used with the Time-out Card to help him expel some of his feelings in a safe way.

Helpful Contacts and Further Reading

Leeds Youth Offending Service (Training for group work: D'Fuse programme) 31 Moor Road, Leeds, LS6 4BG. Tel: 0113 214 4650.

Browne, D., Clarke, S. and McCaffrey, T. (2003) *D'Fuse*. Leeds: Leeds Youth Offending Team.

Faupel, A., Herrick, E. and Sharp, P. (1998) *Anger Management*. London: David Fulton Publishers.

Williams, E. and Barlow, R. (2001) *Anger Control Training*. Bicester: Speechmark Publishing Ltd.

Beware: Anger Bomb!

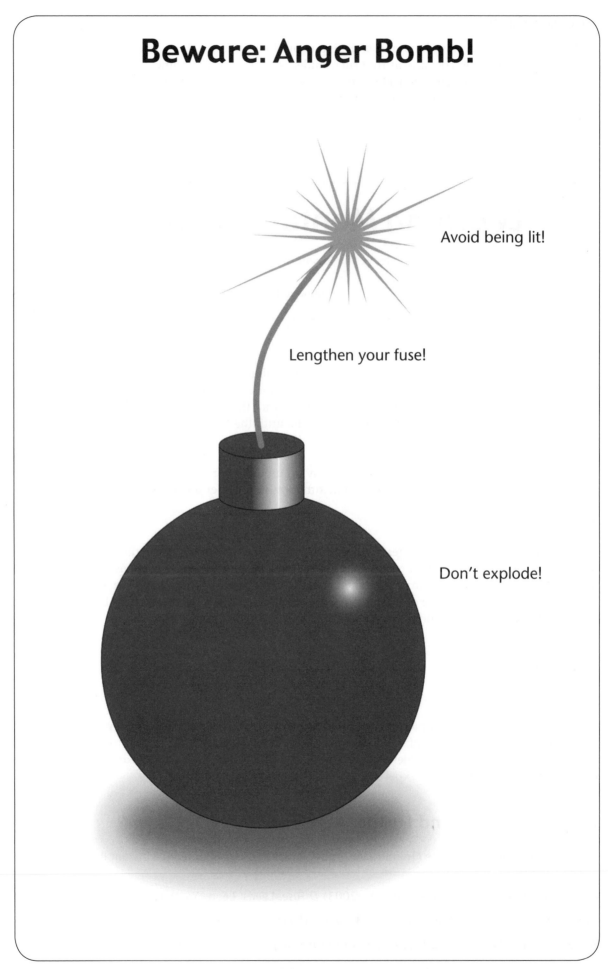

Avoid being lit!

Lengthen your fuse!

Don't explode!

Anger Pie

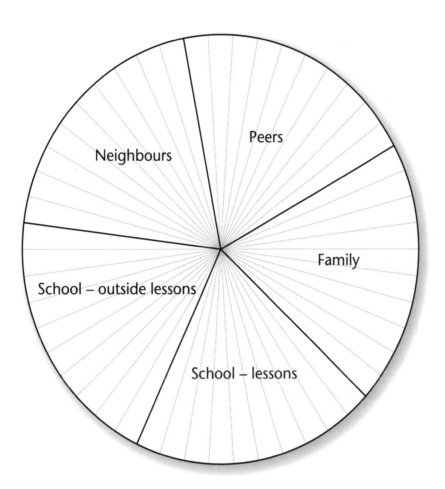

Score yourself from 0 to 10 according to how angry you feel in these five different situations (0 means not angry at all, 10 means furious!)

Peers ☐
Neighbours ☐
School (outside lessons) ☐
School (lessons) ☐
Family ☐

Now colour in the pie chart according to how high you've scored yourself. So if you have given yourself a 10, colour the whole section, if you have given yourself a 5, colour half of it. If you have given yourself a 0, leave it blank.

What Makes You Angry?

Tick the boxes next to each situation that applies to you.
There are some blank spaces for you to fill in if the reason isn't here.

- ☐ Getting told off for something I haven't done.
- ☐ Someone calling members of my family names.
- ☐ Someone calling me names.
- ☐ Someone calling my friends names.
- ☐ Being shouted at.
- ☐ A friend telling someone one of my secrets.
- ☐ Not being able to do the work I have been given.
- ☐ People talking about me behind my back.
- ☐ If something is unfair.
- ☐ If someone pushes me.
- ☐ If someone threatens me.
- ☐ Making a mistake.
- ☐ If a friend does something wrong and then blames me.
- ☐ If someone grasses on me.
- ☐ Getting an answer wrong.
- ☐ Not being allowed to do what I want.
- ☐ _____
- ☐ _____
- ☐ _____
- ☐ _____
- ☐ _____

Now decide which three make you the angriest and underline or highlight them. The situations you ticked are your triggers. These are the things that light your fuse! The situations you underlined or highlighted are the triggers you react most to.

The Learning Mentor's Resource Book
Student use | Chapter Three: Anger Management
Photocopy or print from CD-ROM

10-16

Thoughts – Feelings – Actions

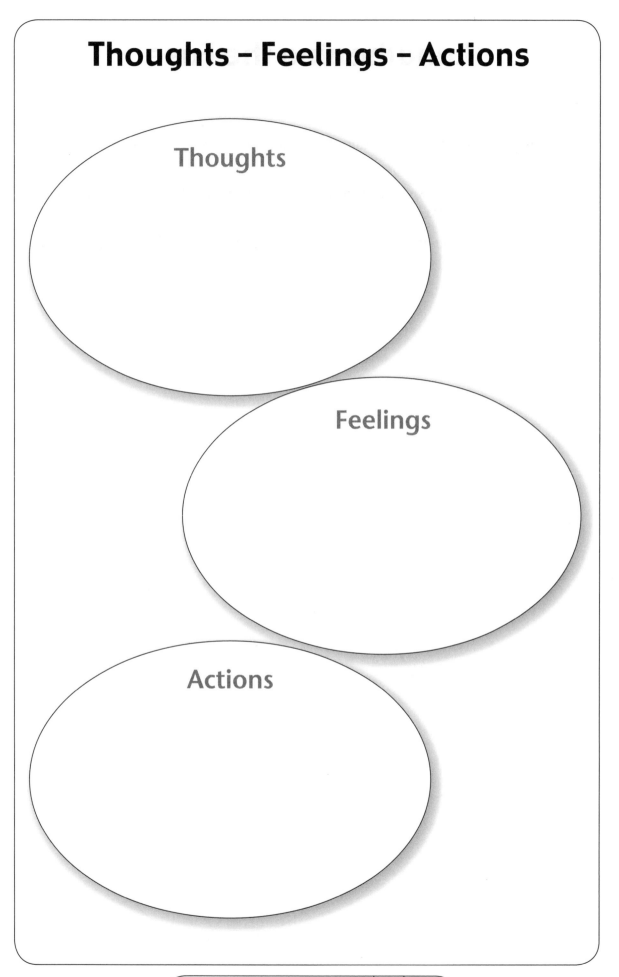

Thoughts

Feelings

Actions

Lengthening the Fuse

Our thoughts lead us to feel certain things, and our feelings cause us to do certain things.

If you can change the way you think about your triggers, then you can feel better about them and be less likely to react angrily.

When you do this you are lengthening your fuse, making the bomb less likely to explode.

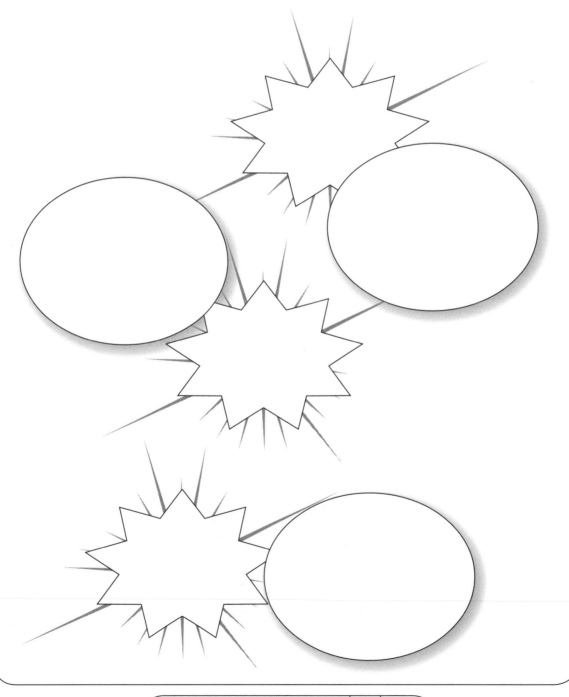

Putting Out the Flame

Strategies to Control Anger

1. Practise these techniques.
2. Decide which ones will be most useful to you.
3. Keep practising them so you don't forget them when needed.

Catchphrase

Decide on a particular phrase to say to yourself in situations where you feel angry.
Practise it and then repeat it in your head over and over again when your feel angry.

Deep Breathing with Pleasant Thoughts

1. Close your eyes.
2. Take a deep breath through your nose.
3. Breathe out through your mouth imaging a pleasant scene.
4. Describe to yourself the smells, sounds, colours...

Talk Sense to Yourself

1. Recognise when you are starting to feel angry.
2. Talk yourself through the feelings using phrases such as:
   ...I know I'll be OK...
   ...Stay calm...
   ...There's no point getting angry...
   ...It will not last forever...

Breathing Control

1. Breathe in through your nose: calm, quick breaths.
2. Breathe out through your mouth.
3. Say a word to yourself each time, such as 'calm' or 'relax'.

Deep Breathing Counting Backwards

1. Take a deep breath through your nose.
2. Breathe out through your mouth saying 'ten'.
3. Repeat saying 'nine'.
4. Repeat to '0'.

Retracking

Retrack incidents that have not gone well.
Talk through the situation, changing key actions, stating what the alternative outcome could be.

Counting to 'Ten'

When you feel yourself getting angry in a situation, do not open your mouth to respond in any way until you have counted to ten.

Stop, Think, Do

When you are in a difficult situation, remember this:

- Stop
- Think
- Do

Thoughts Stopping

1. Practise thinking negative thoughts.
2. When someone says 'stop', make your thoughts positive.

7–11 Breathing

1. Breathe in through the mouth for a count of seven.
2. Breathe out though the nose for a count of 11.

Time-out

Practise using a time-out card, and arrange where you would go if you had to remove yourself from a lesson.

Physical Anger

Mark on the body outline where you feel your anger in your body.

Anger Line

Where on the line are you now?

Least angry   **Most angry**

1 2 3 4 5 6 7 8 9 10

Why are you at this number?

How do you feel now?

What can you do to lower the number?

How do you feel now?

Are you calm enough to return to your lesson?

☐ Yes   ☐ No

Why?

Chapter Four
BEREAVEMENT

Introduction

Experiencing bereavement is difficult, confusing and emotional. It can be acutely distressing for young people, particularly if the deceased person is a parent or caregiver. This chapter offers guidance about how to support a young person through bereavement. Some children may need specialist support but for most, simply being there and caring makes a difference. Within the school environment, it is important to communicate with the family and ensure that they and their young person agree with the proposed support. It is useful to identify a named 'supporter' amongst the staff as the student may need to build a trusting relationship with one person if he is to engage in opportunities to express his feelings, communicate thoughts and to remember. Often, this is the role of the learning mentor as she is generally more easily accessible than a teaching member of staff but it may be a teacher who the student already has a relationship with. It is important that the student can seek his supporter whenever needed in addition to any scheduled sessions. The appointed supporter needs to develop an awareness of any issues that may surround the individual circumstances of the bereavement, including cultural differences in dealing with death.

Adults and parents often assume that a counselling approach is needed. However, secure relationships within the family can act as a resilience factor and children may not want to talk about their loss with a 'stranger' or anyone outside the family. If this is the young person's wish, it should be accepted and empowering a family member to support appropriately can be helpful. Research and anicdotal feedback from young people suggest that it is vital to be clear about the facts and use language such as 'death' and 'dying' as opposed to 'passed away', 'expired' or 'gone to heaven'. Younger children in particular may misunderstand these descriptions and invent fantasies that can damage the grieving process; a sense of involvement and an understanding can help move them through the stages of grief. Where possible, establishing a strong liaison with home is paramount. Family members will have their own grief to cope with so sensitivity is clearly needed. The family may want advice regarding access to bereavement support agencies, how to support the child and feedback on his progress in school.

Remember the individuality of both the circumstances and the student; some will respond best to talking, many to creative work such as drawing and others may simply require support in the form of 'being there' and focusing on something different. Assess and respond to the student's needs, allowing him to determine the nature of support. Spending time as determined by the student with a ready listener is the key to successful support. Most young people will ultimately manage their grief with this level of support but if the family identifies a change in the student's behaviour, such as in conduct or bed-wetting, that continues over a period of time beyond the death, this may indicate a more complicated response to grief and require a referral for extra or more specialist advice (Worden, 2002). Most Child and Adolescent Mental Health Services will offer guidance on the suitability to refer.

Worksheets

Bereavement Response Plan

The Bereavement Response Plan was inspired by an article in *Spotlight* (2003). It is adaptable to fit individual circumstances and school procedures. Discussions should be held between immediate staff, such as the Head of Year and Form Tutor, and the family to decide what information classmates should be given and to confirm that all staff are made aware so they can acknowledge and respond sensitively to the death. Most young people need their loss to be acknowledged by staff and peers alike, whilst trying to maintain some level of normal routine. The class teacher may wish to explore with the class how they can support the student – this may include giving space as well as companionship. The basic theme of the Bereavement Response Plan is to appoint a specified supporter who will see the student on her return to school to check out what support and response she would prefer and to establish a relationship in which she can explore and manage her grief.

Bereavement Booklet

Drawing is a very powerful form of communication, especially for young people who may find it less intrusive than talking. The worksheets can form a short booklet for the student to work through in sessions with his supporter. As an initial task, the student could design a front cover for the booklet as an introduction to this style of intervention; this also generates ownership. The student then works through each activity. The idea is for the student to draw whatever image he thinks of in response to each sentence. Ask the student open questions about the picture such as, 'What have you drawn here?' or, 'Can you tell me a little about this part?' prompting further discussion. If a student is unwilling to draw, he can write his response – some students worry about not being talented at drawing but the booklet is not intended to be aesthetically pleasing! The pace of working through the booklet should be set by the student, but it is important to take some time over it to cover any issues raised in depth. Explore questions and uncertainties about death with a factual and sensitive response. It is also important to be aware about any cultural beliefs. The student may wish to keep his booklet once finished, which is encouraged.

My Support Circle

Losing somebody close can feel very isolating to a young person. This is located in Chapter Five and can help the student identify whom she can ask for support. There are three circles. The inner circle closest to 'me' is where the student writes the names of those who are closest to her, and can offer a lot of support. This could include family, or close friends. The next circle is for those who support her, such as other friends, an adult she can talk to, and possibly yourself. The outer circle is for those in the community who could offer support, such as a doctor or counsellor. It is more interesting for the student to use lots of colour with this worksheet.

Activities

Memory Box

This is a creative way for the student to positively remember the deceased person and to generate discussion. You will need craft materials for this activity. It may help to generate ideas of what the student wants the box to represent, what it could contain and how she wishes to remember the person prior to actually making it. The student decorates a cardboard box, such as a shoebox, in any way she wishes – sometimes in the person's favorite colour or as an image such as the night sky. The student can then bring in any items they want to be in the box including letters, objects and photos. Another idea is to create a fact file for the person including favorite things, hobbies, likes and dislikes. She may wish to draw pictures or write a story of her memories.

If the student is moving house following the death, this box is a good way of symbolising that memories follow wherever she goes.

You may feel it appropriate to liaise with the student's family or carers regarding permission for this activity.

Sculpting

This activity requires a selection of objects such as shells, stones, fruit or a range of plastic animals. Ask the student to choose one of the shells, fruit or animals to represent himself and give two reasons why; for example, two characteristics he 'shares' with the object. Then ask the student to choose which object represents the deceased person. You could repeat this for other family members if appropriate or for different 'types' of memories. This idea could incorporate many different themes ranging from cars to colours to flowers and could be drawn if physical objects are unavailable. It may be helpful to use an area of interest to the child.

Star

It is recommended that you search Internet sites for inspiration. An excellent one is Winston's Wish (see Helpful Contacts). A good interactive task on the site is a night sky in which bereaved children can add a star for the deceased person, with the person's name and any memories they wish to share.

Helpful Contacts and Further Reading

www.winstonswish.org.uk

www.ncb.org.uk/cbn

www.childbereavement.org.uk The Child Bereavement Charity. Tel: 01494 446648

www.childdeathhelpline.org.uk Child Death Helpline. Tel: 0800 282986 (Freephone; Language Line available for interpretation)

www.tcf.org.uk The Compassionate Friends (TCF) – support for parents, grandparents and siblings or www.siblingsupport.org.uk Helpline: 0845 1232304

www.crusebereavementcare.org.uk

www.rd4u.org.uk (for young people)

www.bluecross.org.uk Pet bereavement support line. Tel: 0800 0966606

www.notredamecentre.org.uk Seasons for Growth (a loss and bereavement education programme for children aged 6–18 years)

www.samm.org.uk Support after Murder and Manslaughter (SAMM). Tel: 0845 8723440 (includes telephone interpreting services)

Murray Parkes, C. (2006) *Love and Loss: The Roots of Grief and its Complications*. London: Routledge.

Worden, J. W. (2002) *Children and Grief: When a Parent Dies*. New York: The Guilford Press.

Bereavement Response Plan

- All Staff should be made aware of the death and this should be viewed as confidential. Staff more closely involved with the young person, such as the Head of Year, From Tutor and Learning Mentor, should discuss his/her support plan.

- A letter of condolence is sent out to the family. It should include local child bereavement helplines and contacts. See the contacts list at the end of the introduction for organisations that can help provide these.

- The Head of Year or the nominated person is to telephone family (where relevant) to communicate what is happening in school.

- The Form Tutor, with the support of the Head of Year, should talk to the form class about how the bereaved young person may be feeling and how the class will support him/her on their return to school. The class could discuss how they might respond to the young person and the feelings connected with loss and grief. Be aware of anyone in the form who this event may affect.

- The nominated adult supporter, preferably chosen by the child, meets the young person as they arrive back to school to spend time together. This also allows time and space for the nominated supporter to inform the child of developments in school.

- Ensure that the young person understands that he/she may leave lessons to seek out their chosen supporter in addition to scheduled sessions. Staff should be made aware of this.

- There should be time set aside at the end of their first day back to see their nominated supporter.

- Provide scheduled sessions between the nominated person and the student to explore and support the grieving process.

- The relevant persons should be made aware of the funeral date. A representative for the school may wish to attend.

- Identify if any extra support is needed such as time out of lessons to spend in a suitable environment such as a learning support unit.

- Within support sessions, compile a 'calendar of memories' with dates that the young person may find particularly difficult. If a young person has lost their father, for example, then the anniversary of his death, his birthday and Father's Day may be times this young person requires extra support. This calendar can follow the child through school.

- Staff that teach the child should identify any areas of heightened sensitivity for the child, for example, if they lost a parent in a fire, studying the Great Fire of London may be difficult.

- Closely monitor the young person's progress ensuring support and maintaining contact with the family.

The Learning Mentor's Resource Book	
Facilitator use	Chapter Four: Bereavement
Photocopy or print from CD-ROM	

!

87

Bereavement Booklet

Change is natural. It happens to everybody, every day.

Draw something you like about…

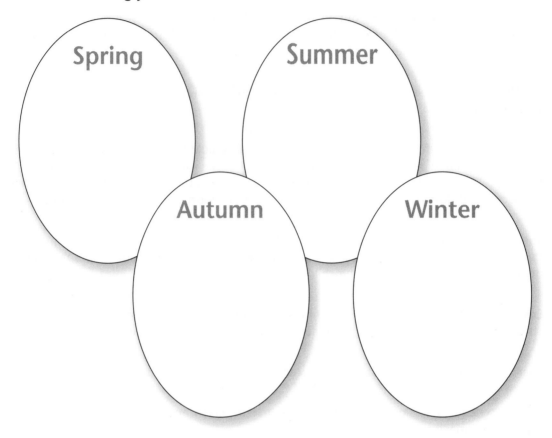

Spring

Summer

Autumn

Winter

Life changes

My life when
I was born

My life today

My life in twenty
years' time

Sometimes change brings good things

Sometimes change brings not so good things

Life is a bit like the sea. Sometimes it can be calm and smooth. Sometimes it can be rough and stormy.

Draw a picture of a stormy sea.

Draw a picture of a calm sea.

Which picture of the sea is your life like right now?

The Learning Mentor's Resource Book		
Student use	Chapter Four: Bereavement	10-16
Photocopy or print from CD-ROM		

89

Life Changes All the Time

Death is the last change in life. That means death is the end of living. Draw what death means to you...

Somebody special to me died. Draw a picture of your special person...

There are Lots of Different Beliefs About What Happens When Somebody Dies

Draw some of the different beliefs that you know...

What I think happens...

Things I Don't Know About Death and Might Like to Ask Somebody...

(lined writing space)

This is Me Saying, 'Goodbye' to My Special Person...

(blank space)

The Learning Mentor's Resource Book

Student use | Chapter Four: Bereavement

Photocopy or print from CD-ROM

10-16

Sometimes People Hide Their Real Feelings and Pretend Different Feelings to Others

Draw some feelings that people might hide...

How I am feeling...

Good Ways to Get My Feelings Out...

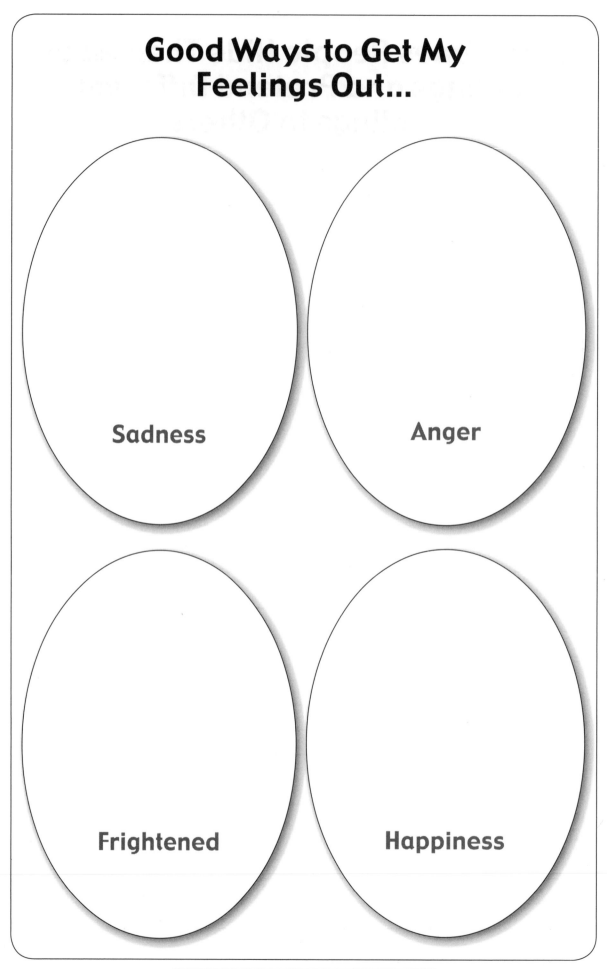

Sadness

Anger

Frightened

Happiness

The Learning Mentor's Resource Book

Student use | Chapter Four: Bereavement

Photocopy or print from CD-ROM

10-16

Things That Make Me
Feel Better...

Something Positive
About Me...

The Learning Mentor's Resource Book		
Student use	Chapter Four: Bereavement	10-16
Photocopy or print from CD-ROM		

95

My Special Person Taught Me Something Important...

_____
_____
_____
_____
_____
_____
_____
_____
_____
_____
_____
_____
_____

Good Memories Are Mine to Keep...

_____
_____
_____
_____
_____
_____
_____
_____
_____
_____
_____
_____
_____
_____
_____

It is OK to Still Have Fun!

This is me having happy times...

The Learning Mentor's Resource Book		
Student use	Chapter Four: Bereavement	
Photocopy or print from CD-ROM		

10-16

97

Chapter Five
SELF-HARM

Introduction

Self-harm has often been regarded as attention seeking and viewed as being of rare occurrence, but self-harm in young people is becoming increasingly common. It is impossible to say exactly how many young people self-harm because of the secrecy surrounding the behaviour. Many young people take a considerable amount of time before they find the courage to tell someone and many actually never seek counselling or medical help. The Mental Health Foundation said in their 2006 report *Truth Hurts* that at least 1 in 15 children and young people self harm, beginning at an average age of 12. It would appear to be more common in girls than boys, but this may be due to under reporting. It is also important to note that the rates of self-harm reported by parents are much lower than the rates of self-harm reported by children, suggesting that many parents are unaware that their children are self-harming (see www.selfharm.org.uk). This highlights the issue of confidentiality. Ensure that you are fully aware of your school's confidentiality policy and where issues of self-harm lie within it. Talk to the teacher responsible for Safeguarding (Child Protection), and identify with them at which point you should inform them of a self-harm disclosure (some self-harm behaviours are relatively minor, and may be dealt with initially within the mentoring relationship – see below for behaviours to watch out for), and make sure you always communicate this to young people *before* they are likely to tell you any information. If the self-harm is serious we always advise the young person that we will contact home and then inform parents or carers about our concerns regarding the self-harm and that young person's safety. If you are ever unsure of the level of risk, it is *always* advisable to contact the young person's home and your child protection officer. It is *always* serious if a young person is using some sort of implement or substance with which to hurt themselves.

Self-harm behaviours can include: nail biting, hair-pulling (to various degrees), skin chewing or scratching, tattooing, banging walls with parts of the body, stabbing, cutting, swallowing toxic substances, swallowing other objects, deliberate overdosing (self-poisoning), burning or scalding, jumping off heights or into moving traffic, causing a fight, inserting objects, or putting oneself into deliberate danger or risky situations.

Self-harm is very personal. The meaning varies for each individual and can also differ for each occurrence. If you are supporting a young person who self-harms, it is vital that you simply listen to her. Although you may be working with her in the boundaries of school hours it is also helpful for the young person if she is able to approach you outside any scheduled sessions. This means that if she is in school and struggling at any point, she can access support.

It is important to show recognition of self-harm as a coping strategy and to encourage the young person to see her self-harm as a sign of emotion that needs to be expressed. Initially, support the young person in understanding her self-harm by exploring meanings, emotions and triggers behind their self-harm. The worksheets in this section are designed to help you do this. You can also help the young person to look for safer ways of expressing her feelings and explore alternative coping strategies. Again this will be very individual.

In many cases, you may find it beneficial to also do some self-esteem work with the young person, as this can often be very low. Some young people also benefit from emotional intelligence work to help them recognise the emotions that are fuelling the self-harm, as many young people find it difficult to express themselves emotionally. Encouraging the student to write letters or keep a journal will familiarise her with externalising emotion, which can also work as an alternative coping strategy. The young person may wish to bring any letters or journals in for you to read from which you can discuss any feelings or triggers that have been recorded. It is important for the young person to be aware that your confidentiality policy applies also to written information.

Worksheets

Prochaska and Diclemente's Six Stages of Change

Prochaska and Diclemente's cognitive process of change cycle (Prochaska et al., 1995) is relevant to understanding the behaviour change cycle, which the young person is likely to go through. The different stages are described in relation to self-harming behaviour. It highlights that even when a young person is making positive progress with the self-harm, there is the possibility of relapse.

This tool can be very useful for young people to understand their progress. It can also be used to explain the behavioural changes to parents.

Helpful Responses to Self-harm

This resource reminds you, as a mentor, what information is useful to the student, but more importantly can be used as a worksheet for the student to identify what she relates to. If you are using it with parents or carers, this can be part of an information pack you could send home. It is also a good idea to source some information leaflets for parents from the other contacts at the end of the introduction to this chapter.

What Functions Does Self-harm Provide?

Again, this is a useful worksheet to send to parents or carers to encourage their understanding of what their child is experiencing. Additionally, this can be used with young people to initially explain the many different reasons behind self-harm and help them realise its significance as a coping strategy. Later, it can be used to help the young person identify what purpose their self-harm is serving, which would follow work about triggers (see later activity).

Positive Thinking

This is more of a self-esteem resource and encourages the student to have greater awareness of her positive thoughts. When a student is self-harming, she will dwell on negative emotions. It can also be used to record when the student felt the urge to self-harm but 'resisted', which is positive in itself, especially if they used an alternative strategy. The student records at least one positive thought that she had on that particular day – this can include such things as receiving a compliment, doing well at school or doing a helpful deed. The purpose of the circle for each day is for the young person to bring the worksheet back to you when completed and to receive some form of recognition for her positive thoughts. This could be a sticker, a smiley face, or anything to which the student may respond. It also encourages familiarisation with inner thoughts.

Self-harm: Myths and Facts

This can be used as another tool for providing information for parents. It also develops the student's understanding of self-harm as behaviour and aims to quash fears or misconceptions he may have. It can also help the self-harm seem more 'real'.

My Support Circle

This is to help the student identify whom she can ask for support. There are three circles. The inner circle closest to 'me' is where the student writes the names of those who are closest to her and can offer a lot of support. This could include family or close friends. The next circle is for those who support her, such as other friends, an adult she can talk to and possibly yourself. The outer circle is for those in the community who could offer support, such as a doctor or counsellor. It is more interesting for the student to use lots of colour with this worksheet.

Triggers

This aims to encourage the student to think about what different things may have triggered a self-harm episode. It can be used repeatedly after different episodes, and may identify a pattern of triggers. You can then discuss and explore the triggers and related feelings once they have been identified. At this point, you could also use the Emotion Cards (see Chapter One).

Alternatives

This worksheet provides a fairly comprehensive list of different alternatives that the student may find useful in attempting to refrain from self-harming when he feels an urge to do so. It is worth noting that you may need to edit this list if you feel there are some inappropriate alternatives for the individual with whom you are working. If a student harms for the sensation, then squeezing ice-cubes may be suitable, however this will not help someone self-harming for comfort – a hot bath may be of benefit to him. The two bullet points at the end are for the student to add his own ideas. The extreme alternatives can be supported as a stage towards meeting the student's needs in a more appropriate way.

My Alternative Agreement

Some of the sections on this sheet will be easier to fill in after completing the previous worksheets. Try to increase the number of alternatives that the student is prepared to try. She could be encouraged to eventually be making her way twice through the list to stave off the urge to self-harm. It is important, contractually, that the young person 'signs' to agree, however, to maintain anonymity on the piece of paper, she can put some sort of symbol in the agreement box that signifies her, rather than an actual signature.

Helpful Contacts and Further Reading

http://freespace.virgin.net/basement.project/default.htm

www.nshn.co.uk

www.selfharmalliance.org

www.thesite.org/healthandwellbeing/mentalhealth/selfharm

www.trichotillomania.co.uk/

www.youngminds.org.uk

Bailey, S. and Shooter, M. (2009) *The Young Mind*. London: Bantam Press.

Fox, C. and Hawton, K. (2004) *Deliberate Self-Harm in Adolescence (Child and Adolescent Mental Health)*. London: Jessica Kingsley Publishers.

Mental Health Foundation (2006) *Truth Hurts Report*. Free to download from: http://www.mental-health.org.uk

Middleton, K. and Garvey, S. (2008) *Self Harm: The Path to Recovery*. Oxford: Lion Publishing Plc.

Prochaska, J., Norcross, J. and Diclemente, C. (1995) *Changing for Good*. New York: Perenial Currents.

Spandler, H. and Warner, S. (2007) *Beyond Fear and Control: Working with Young People Who Self Harm*. PCCS Books Ltd: Ross-on-Wye.

Prochaska and Diclemente's Six Stages of Change

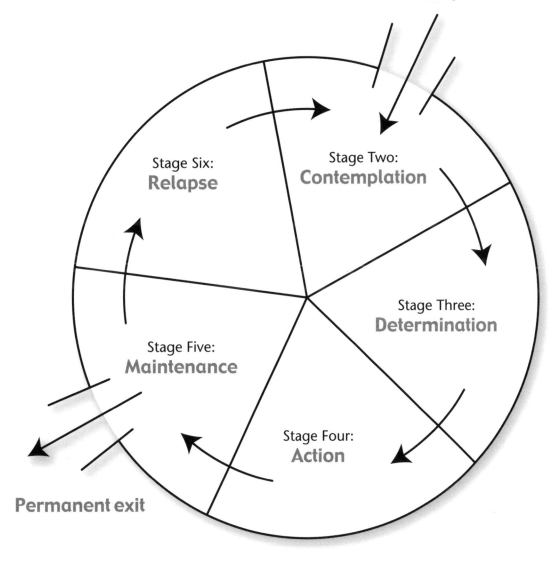

Stage One:
Pre-contemplation

Stage Six:
Relapse

Stage Two:
Contemplation

Stage Three:
Determination

Stage Five
Maintenance

Stage Four:
Action

Permanent exit

Helpful Responses to Self–harm

Listen.
Understand that self-harm is a coping strategy, a way of surviving for that person.
Recognise the need to self-harm and the feelings of distress leading to it.
Show that you see the person behind the self-harm, not just the behaviour.
Have concern for the actual injuries.
Let the young person know it is OK to talk about their self-harm and that it is something that can be understood.
Explore meanings and feelings behind the self-harm, to encourage the young person's understanding.
Explore the triggers – this will help the young person understand and discover alternatives that are best suited to them as an individual.
Encourage the young person to see self-harm as a signal of buried feelings that need to be expressed.
Help the young person to develop other methods of expressing these feelings.
Explore alternative coping strategies to self-harm and the understanding that these will differ depending upon the person and the different triggers.
Support and acknowledge each small step as a major achievement.
Don't make stopping self-harm the most important goal or a condition of your support.

102

The Learning Mentor's Resource Book
Facilitator use | Chapter Five: Self-harm
Photocopy or print from CD-ROM

!

What Functions Does Self-harm Provide?

- Used to cope with a distressing life event(s).

- Way of dealing with abuse, neglect, losing somebody important through death or otherwise, being bullied or harassed, being assaulted, being very lonely or isolated and other such difficult feelings.

- Escapism – feel unreal or numb.

- Expression of emotions that the young person does not understand, cannot recognize or is unable to verbalise.

- Release of unbearable feelings.

- Self-punishment, meaning getting rid of 'badness'.

- Gain sense of control over body.

- Express distress to others.

- Taking care of injuries afterwards can bring sense of comfort and being cared for.

- To block out emotional pain with physical pain.

- Release from emotional intensity.

- Release from feeling numb or empty, to feel 'alive'.

The Learning Mentor's Resource Book		
Facilitator use	Chapter Five: Self-harm	**!**
Photocopy or print from CD-ROM		

103

Positive Thinking

Day		
Monday		
Tuesday		
Wednesday		
Thursday		
Friday		
Saturday		
Sunday		

The Learning Mentor's Resource Book
Student use | Chapter Five: Self-harm
Photocopy or print from CD-ROM

12-16

Self-harm: Myths and Facts

Myth:

Self-harm is just a way of attention seeking.

Myth:

Self-harm is rare in young people.

Myth:

People who self-harm are trying to kill themselves.

Myth:

Young people self-harm for no good reason.

Myth:

Young people self-harm over trivial reasons.

Myth:

People who self-harm are mad.

Myth:

Self-harm which is superficial is not 'serious'.

Myth:

Self-harm is only about cutting yourself.

Myth:

Once you have self-harmed you cannot stop.

The Learning Mentor's Resource Book		
Facilitator use	Chapter Five: Self-harm	
Photocopy or print from CD-ROM		

!

105

Self-harm: Myths and Facts

Fact:

Self-harm is a coping strategy. People self-harm because they are finding something difficult and painful. They could also be trying to show that something is wrong. They need to be taken seriously.

Fact:

Lots of people self-harm. There is lots of secrecy around self-harm and because many young people do not tell anyone, it is hard to know exactly how many are self-harming. The Royal College of Psychiatrists (1999) found that as many as 1 in 10 teenagers have deliberately self-harmed.

Fact:

Sometimes people do harm themselves because they want to die. But more often than not, it's about staying alive. Young people may self-harm to help them cope through a bad time.

Fact:

All self-harm should be treated seriously. People self-harm to different extremes as it is a coping strategy and everybody is unique. The extent of the self-harm is not necessarily a reflection of how serious the personal difficulties are.

Fact:

People can self-harm just one or twice. Some use self-harm over a long period of time. The frequency of the self-harm varies. Many people do stop self-harming but only when they are ready. This could be when they sort their problems out or when they find other ways to deal with their feelings.

Fact:

Lots of different people self-harm. It does not mean they are mad. It is a sign that they are trying to cope with something difficult and upsetting.

Fact:

People self-harm in different ways. Self-harm can include cutting different parts of the body, burning, biting, scratching, banging, bruising and pulling hair. Some people take tablets, maybe not enough to overdoes but enough to forget their problems for a while. Things such as starving, overeating, taking drugs, smoking and risk-taking can also be 'self-harm'. Some coping strategies, for example, excessive exercise or burying themselves in their work, can seem more acceptable, but can still be harmful.

The Learning Mentor's Resource Book
Facilitator use | Chapter Five: Self-harm
Photocopy or print from CD-ROM

!

My Support Circle

Triggers

Mark the triggers below which you feel applied to you at that time...

☐ I argued with a friend.	☐ I got stressed with...
☐ A teacher shouted at me.	☐ I was under pressure.
☐ Somebody insulted me.	☐ I wanted to take my mind off something else...
☐ I argued with someone in my family.	☐ Somebody touched/pushed me.
☐ I got into trouble.	☐ I wanted to cause myself pain.
☐ A friend left me out.	☐ I was being bullied.
☐ Something on TV upset me.	☐ Some one shouted at me.
☐ I got a bad mark at school.	☐ I got into a fight.
☐ I did something I shouldn't have.	☐ I couldn't express how I felt inside.
☐ I thought about a specific incident.	☐ People in my house argued with each other.
☐ I drank some alcohol.	☐ I didn't like myself.
☐ I thought about somebody.	☐ I thought I was unsafe.
☐ I felt bad about myself.	☐ I missed somebody.
☐ I was reminded of a specific incident.	☐ I listened to some music that upset me.
☐ Nobody understood me.	☐ I wanted somebody to notice how bad I feel inside.
☐ Someone wasn't listening to me.	☐ I wanted somebody to help me.
☐ I felt bad about the way I look.	☐ I wanted to feel myself again.
☐ I felt bad about my body.	☐ _____
☐ I thought that somebody didn't love me.	☐ _____
☐ Someone embarrassed me.	☐ _____
☐ I felt low about my personality.	☐ _____
☐ Someone got more attention than me.	

The Learning Mentor's Resource Book

Student use | Chapter Five: Self-harm

Photocopy or print from CD-ROM

12-16

Alternatives

- [ ] Go out for a walk (when safe).

- [ ] Ring a friend.

- [ ] Talk to somebody.

- [ ] Get out of the house. For example, into your garden or yard for fresh air.

- [ ] Write a letter or diary.

- [ ] Draw or paint feelings.

- [ ] Rip up old paper or material if angry.

- [ ] Listen to music – appropriate songs, positive music!

- [ ] Go to bed, sleep.

- [ ] Squeeze ice cubes.

- [ ] Hand in bucket of icy water (not for too long).

- [ ] Wear rubber band loosely around wrist and flick it against skin.

- [ ] Draw marks on self with red pen or paint or use henna tattoos.

- [ ] Buy inflatable baseball bat and whack pillows.

- [ ] Bite into something strongly flavoured, for example, a lemon or chilli pepper.

- [ ] Make an appointment with mentor or doctor or counsellor.

- [ ] Hug a teddy bear.

- [ ] Talk to somebody from your Support Circle.

- [ ] Ring ChildLine: 0800 1111 Or email, chat or text – see www.childline.org.uk Ring Samaritans: 08457 909090

- [ ] Read a book or magazine.

- [ ] Have a cold shower.

- [ ] Have a hot bath to relax.

- [ ] Carry a stone, stress ball or something similar in your pocket to rub, squeeze or play with.

- [ ] Reality checks – count things in the room, study the colours of your surroundings and give yourself a running description of everything surrounding you.

- [ ] Give yourself a task to do, such as tidying your room.

- [ ] Do an activity or hobby you usually enjoy.

- [ ] Exercise or do something energetic – running, football, swimming, gym, dancing, tennis, yoga...

- [ ] _____

- [ ] _____

- [ ] _____

My Alternative Agreement

Situations when I am most likely to harm myself:

Feelings I may have when I am most likely to harm myself:

What I do when I harm myself:

People in my Support Circle who I can talk to:

Alternatives I can try when I feel the urge to hurt myself:

I agree that before I self-harm I will try to do at least _____ of my alternatives above.

Agreement Box

The Learning Mentor's Resource Book

Student use | Chapter Five: Self-harm

Photocopy or print from CD-ROM

13-16

Chapter Six
DRUG AWARENESS

Introduction

The term 'drug' covers a wide range of substances from medical prescriptions to cigarettes, from alcohol to heroin. As indicated, some drugs are legal and others illegal. Everyone will face different situations in their lives when they come into contact with drugs, whether this is being persuaded to try a cigarette or being offered cocaine at a party. The choice is then ultimately down to that person. This chapter aims to address drug use involving illegal drugs as opposed to cigarettes and alcohol, simply as there seems to be more of a demand for ideas on how to work with young people in this area. Therefore, provided are some suggestions on how to support young people in relation to drug awareness and some possible worksheets to support this. It is a difficult area to address in a book, as the information needs regularly updating. For example, in recent years cannabis has been reclassified and suppliers often try to produce new chemical mixes that can be sold as a 'legal high'. A recent example of this is Mephedrone (or MCAT) which was sold as plant food before being made illegal as a class B drug in 2010 after a number of deaths were associated with the drug. You are therefore advised to seek the most current and young-person-friendly information from the Helpful Contacts at the end of this section. It is also worth considering what is applicable within different cultures and countries; in the USA crystal-meth is a significant problem but it is less common in the UK.

A harm reduction perspective is taken in this book, as young people tend to relate to this attitude more efficiently – it is not very often you can tell a young person not to do something and they don't. It is still vital, however, to give the young person a clear message regarding how dangerous drugs can be. It is important to ensure this complies with your school's drug education policy and be very aware of how the disclosure of drug use fits into your confidentiality statement. In some establishments, if a student admits to having used cannabis once or twice but is not doing so now, it may be kept confidential. However, if this is a regular occurrence or involves any drug of a higher classification, then parents and senior management should be informed as this could be a matter of safeguarding the young person. Your confidentiality statement needs to be reiterated with any young person you are supporting, particularly if you feel there may be a drug issue.

Wherever possible, it is advisable to invite a drugs agency into school to work with students on drug awareness. It may be worth checking how this coincides with your school's PHSCE curriculum. These agencies provide a much more knowledgeable and accessible service for young people. Another useful tool is a picture of what the different drugs look like. Again, it is suggested that you contact agencies for these resources, or a drug agency worker may bring such graphics in a session.

The aim of the worksheets and activities is to provide the young person with accurate information about what drugs are and what they can do to you, to enable him to make an informed choice in a situation. Without knowledge, a young person could accept a 'smoke' at a party believing it to be cannabis, when the substance could actually be heroin.

There are two main approaches to working with a student on drug awareness. It could be educational, to provide information in preparation for a possible encounter with drugs. Or you may be supporting someone you suspect is using drugs but this has not been confirmed, or a student who is using drugs and has been caught or openly admits this. In the latter case, remember to ensure that you are complying with your school's drugs policy. Be sensitive to the fact that some young people may come from families in which drugs are used; in which case there are usually local projects which support children of drug users. You may need to enable the student to understand the choice involved in drug use if he sees the use of drugs as condoned or acceptable.

Finally, it is beneficial to display posters and provide leaflets and helpline numbers that advertise projects accessible to young people who may have concerns about drugs or drug use and who may feel too scared to seek direct help.

Worksheets

Slang Names

These sheets intend to further the student's knowledge about names given to different drugs. These lists are not exhaustive and are liable to change frequently. Some terms have been included that may not be a name for the drug but a method of using it, or something strongly associated with it. For example, the term 'rattling' is used in relation to heroin to describe when a user is attempting to detoxify from the drug. As such, the user displays withdrawal symptoms and can be desperate for their next 'fix'. The worksheets could be used to read over and familiarise the student with the various slang names.

It is more interactive to photocopy the names to make word cards and ask the student to place them with their formal name. This is not a test! Even a student with great awareness may not have heard each name, especially considering regional variations. She may wish to add some of her own.

Stimulants, Depressants and Hallucinogens

This sheet provides further exploration of what drugs do to a person and allows the student to further his knowledge on stimulants, depressants and hallucinogens. The terms used are intended to be easy for the student to relate to. A further activity is to then place drug word cards (see above activity) into groups of stimulants, depressants and hallucinogens. This information is generally included in the above worksheets. Ask the student to place alcohol into a category in this activity.

Classification

It is important to make the point that drugs are classified in relation to how dangerous they are.

This is a very simple worksheet as updated information should be sought from an agency. It is suggested that you make word cards (as above) for the formal names that the student can place into each category, generating discussion regarding what makes the student think the drug belongs to that category. This should initiate some discussion of the student's views on the seriousness of each drug. Then place the drugs in the correct categories, if necessary. The current classifications are given in the What Do You Know exercise. But remember to contact a drugs agency or a government website for changes. It is worth noting that many young people have misconceptions about the recent reclassification of cannabis from class C to B and it is beneficial, if not essential, to clearly explain the implications of this.

Penalties and the Law

Again, seek recent guidance from a drug project, government website or your police-school liaison officer regarding the current laws surrounding drugs and the consequences of breaking such laws.

The table is intended to clearly show the maximum penalties for someone charged with possession, or possession with intent to supply. Make sure the student is aware of the difference between 'possession' and 'supply'. Use this opportunity to discuss the effect of having a drugs conviction on record – for example, the student would be restricted from holding certain jobs.

Reasons for Using Drugs

A possible starting point is to discuss how many people the student thinks may use drugs in school, and which substances. This includes how many students they think smoke cigarettes, how many have tried cannabis, how many smoke it regularly and so on. This could be as a number, percentage or fraction.

This can then lead on to a discussion of why young people use drugs. This worksheet can be used generally and also personally for that individual; it is possible to do both by using different colours to circle the responses. The student's answers may then highlight what needs to be addressed or raise further issues that need to be tackled.

Pros and Cons

This worksheet should provoke thought on the advantages and disadvantages of using drugs. Explore these with the student. Again, this could be used generally or on an individual level depending upon what is relevant to the student you are supporting.

My Drug Use Affects...

This is intended to encourage the student to look beyond the effects on themselves and explore who else may be affected by their drug use. Further this by thinking about how it affects each person.

What Do You Know?

This worksheet focuses primarily on cannabis but could be adapted for other drugs. This could be used at the beginning of your work to identify the student's knowledge prior to support, or in conclusion of the sessions to evaluate what has been learned. It also confirms the student's awareness of cannabis and the law, as the issue seems to be misconstrued easily. An answer sheet is provided.

Activities

What is It?

It is suggested that you contact a drug agency such as 'Talk to FRANK' (see Helpful Contacts) who will provide you with informative leaflets giving details about what each drug is, what it does and what the effects are. The leaflets are aimed at young people and are therefore presented in an accessible way. Or you may wish to use drug information cards that most agencies have. Both the leaflet and cards then act as a discussion tool for you to discuss each drug in turn. Involve the student with open questions inviting thought as opposed to reading aloud.

Safety

Develop links with a local drug agency. Explore what the agency offers in terms of conducting drug education in school and exploring the links between drug use and mental health. One aspect they may cover in their sessions is safety – for example, to demonstrate to students the recovery position to help someone who has collapsed. It is vital that students know that they should not leave that person alone, that they must ring an ambulance and inform the medics what the person has taken. It may be worth checking with any colleagues who teach PSHCE/health education for any videos about this topic.

A further possibility of addressing this issue is to invite first-aid workers into school, or approach your school's appointed first-aider.

Using Drama or Media

Invite a drama company in to perform for and work with a group of students as a non-personal way of addressing drug use. They may run a workshop afterwards to explore the characters and issues or hold a question and answer session. Alternatively, you could use an age-appropriate film or TV clip and then discuss the characters feelings, decisions, impact on others and alternative endings.

Helpful Contacts and Further Reading:

National Drug Help Line: 0800 776600

www.drugscope.org.uk

www.hit.org.uk

www.re-solv.org

www.talktofrank.com

www.turning-point.co.uk

www.wrecked.co.uk

Lookadoo, J. (2008) *The Dirt on Drugs*. Michigan: Revell.

Slang Names – Cannabis

Spliff	Dope	Home-grown
Joint	Gear	Hash
Skunk	Rocky	Smoke
Blow	Grass	Herb
Green	Bang	Ganja
Solid	High Grade	Resin
Block	Weed	Squishy
Black	Reefer	Bong
Bush	Draw	Smelly
Bucket	Pot	Sput
Booda	Northern Lights	

Slang Names– Cocaine/Crack Cocaine

Crack	Snow	Powder
Nosebag	Charlie	Rock
Big C	Coke	Snifter
Columbian	Freebase	

Slang Names – Amyl Nitrate

Poppers	Rush	Snappers
TNT	Headrush	Ram

Slang Names – Ketamine

Ket	Kitty Kat	Special K
Vitamin K	Pegasus	Horse

Slang Names – Ecstasy

E	Pills	MDMA
M&Ms	Flatliners	Doves
MDA	Adam	Eve
Chikkas	New Yorkers	Rolexes
XTC	Mitsies	Badboys
Diddlers	Disco Biscuits	

Slang Names – Heroin

Skag	Brown	Gear
Smack	Rattling	H
Shooting up		

Slang Names – Amphetamine

Speed	Amphets	Fet
Meths	Dexies	Base
Whizz	Uppers	Rits
Billy	Bennies	Sulphate

Slang Names – Magic Mushrooms

Mushines	'Shrooms	Trip

Slang Names – Mephedrone

MCAT	Meow	Bubble	Bubbleluv	4MMC
Mieow	Plant food	Discofood	MDMC	

Slang Names – LSD

Tabs	Acid	Strawberries
Blotters	Trip	Microdots

The Learning Mentor's Resource Book
Student use | Chapter Six: Drug Awareness
Photocopy or print from CD-ROM
11-16

Stimulants	Depressants	Hallucinogens
Buzz	Downers	Make you see things
Speed up	Tired	Tripping
Energy	Sleepy	Confused
Nightclubs	Pass out	Unreal
High	Whitey	Think things are happening that aren't
Headrush	Slowed Down	Hear things
Loved up	Chilled	Exaggerates colours, shapes, sounds
Dance all night	Relax	No Control
Thirsty	Throw up	Don't know what is going on
Drink water	Feel sad	Paranoid
Heart beats faster	Gouching	Things speed up
Not hungry	Aggressive	Don't know how long it will last
Upper		Keyhole effect
Comedown		
Aggressive		

Classification

A

B

C

Legal

Penalties and the law

	Possession	Possession with intent to supply or manufacture
Class A	7 years' prison sentence	Life prison sentence Unlimited fine Seizure of assets
Class B	5 years' prison sentences	14 years' prison sentence Unlimited fine Seizure of assets
Class C	2 years' prison sentence	5 years' prison sentence Unlimited fine Seizure of assets

Reasons for Using Drugs

Boredom

Peer pressure

Popularity

Risk taking

Escape from problems

To relax

Something to do

In with the crowd

To feel or look 'big'

To forget things

Curiosity

Can't say 'No'

Dangerous

It's good for us

For the buzz

Solves problems

Calms nerves

Friends do it

Exciting

To get in the mood

Now list the three reasons which you feel are the biggest factors in your drug use.

_____

_____

_____

Pros and Cons

Pros

Cons

My Drug Use Affects...

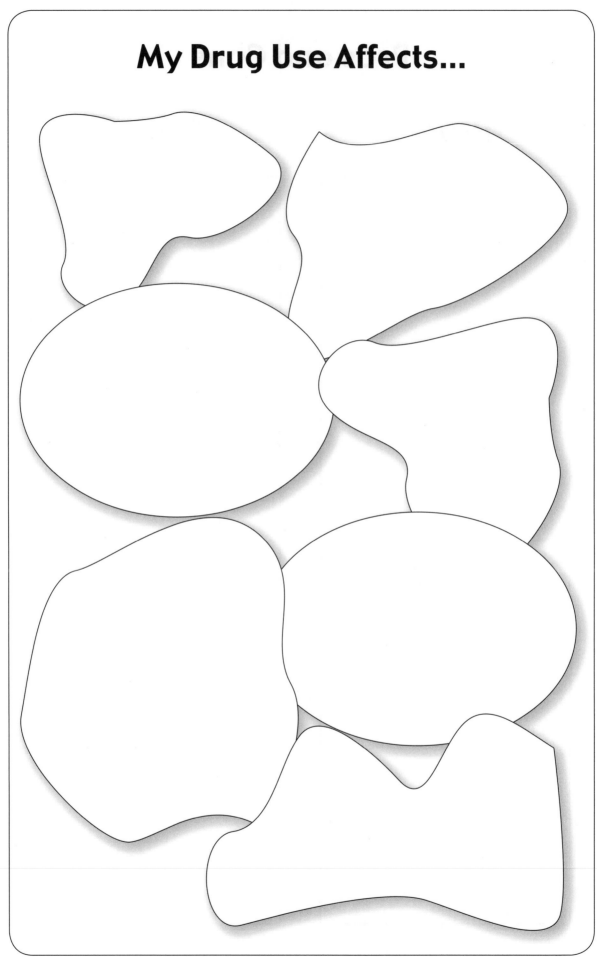

The Learning Mentor's Resource Book

Student use | Chapter Six: Drug Awareness

Photocopy or print from CD-ROM

12-16

What Do You Know?

Cannabis is also known as...

Why does the law classify drugs into three categories?

What are they?

Name three Class A drugs...

1) _____

2) _____

3) _____

'Poppers' are legal in the UK, but why are they dangerous?

What class is cannabis now?

Is it legal to use someone else's prescription drugs?

What can happen if you are caught in possession of cannabis?

Supplying and dealing cannabis is a more serious offence. What is the maximum penalty?

Name three side effects of using cannabis...

1) _____

2) _____

3) _____

Do you know if there are any long-term risks?

What effect could a drugs conviction have on your life?

What Do You Know?
Answer Sheet

1) Cannabis is most commonly known as Weed or a Joint. See the Slang Names sheet for cannabis in this chapter for other names.

2) The three categories reflect the dangerousness of the drug and the severity of the sentence carried in the Legal System.

3) Category A, B and C.

4) Class A – ecstasy, heroin, cocaine, crack cocaine, LSD, magic mushrooms, liquid form amphetamine prepared for injection.
   Class B – amphetamines, cannabis, methylphenidate (ritalin), pholcodine.
   Class C – tranquilisers, some painkillers, gamma hydroxybutyrate (GHB), ketamine.

5) 'Poppers' are extremely poisonous if ingested and drinking the substance can actually kill the person. Sniffing poppers can induce severe headache.

6) Cannabis is a Class B drug.

7) No, it is illegal to use prescription drugs that are prescribed to someone else – they automatically become at least a Class C drug if used by another person.

8) You will be arrested and charged with Possession of an Illegal Drug. If you have a large amount on you, you could be charged with Intent to Supply. The maximum prison sentences for the UK are shown below but check the Home Office website or Talk to Frank if you believe there have been changes.

Class	Maximum for Possession	Maximum for Indent to Supply or Supply
A	Up to 7 years in prison	Up to Life in prison
B	Up to 5 years in prison	Up to 14 years in prison
C	Up to 2 years in prison	Up to 14 years in prison

9) Up to 14 years in prison and/or unlimited fine.

10) Paranoia, weight gain, drowsiness, anger problems, lack of energy, sleep problems – also see the Talk to Frank website.

11) Some research suggests that heavy cannabis use can increase or trigger any underlying mental health problems. The long-term effects of cannabis use are still debated, see Talk to Frank for the most recent guidance. There are the associated long-term health effects from smoking to consider.

12) While there is no set answer to this, any criminal offences on record can prevent people from getting a job, particularly certain jobs such as working for the NHS or working with children. Even spent convictions show up on enhanced Criminal Record Bureau checks.

Chapter Seven
BULLYING

Introduction

A frequent issue that many school staff are expected to deal with is bullying and unfortunately this can be all too prevalent in schools. A bullying policy must by law be in place in all schools, and it is important that anyone aware of bullying takes appropriate action in accordance with this policy.

While some targets of bullying might be unconfident or poor at friendship skills, most are perfectly OK young people. It can happen to anyone and it is important to convey the message to the victim that she is OK and it is not her fault. The behaviour that needs to change is the behaviour of the bully. A focus on victim change implies that the bullying will continue and is therefore a failure in a duty of care.

Most young people who bully are capable of behaving in a positive way and should be supported to change their behaviour. The roles of colluders, observers and rescuers can be addressed to mobilise group dynamics. An effective way to do this is to use the No Blame Support Group Method and details can be found on the Lucky Duck website (www.luckyduck.co.uk).

When procedures are in place to change the behaviour of the bullies this might be sufficient to restore confidence to the target. However, some have suffered significantly and will benefit from activities and learning which could support them in the future should a similar situation arise.

There are many aspects you can address in strengthening the student against bullying. Help the student to recognise the difference between being passive, assertive and aggressive. Often the experience of suffering bullying can lower self-esteem and you may find it beneficial to address this issue – see Chapter Two. In extreme cases, bullying can result in depression, self-harm, school refusal and even running away or suicide attempts. If you have any concerns regarding any such issues, it is essential to discuss this with parents or carers.

There are now concerns about cyber-bullying (bullying over the internet) and text message bullying. These are covered in more detail in the following chapter on internet safety, but mechanisms of support can be very similar to those for other forms of bullying. The main difference is that there may be more anonymity for the person bullying.

Mechanisms of Support

Mobile Phone and Email

A mobile phone number which students can text problems to and receive advice from is a more anonymous method of seeking advice. This could also be achieved with an email service. This does require some thought about time constraints and 'staffing' these facilities.

Peer Support Schemes

You may wish to establish a peer support team within school where students can act as buddies to listen and support the victims of bullying. This could involve older students. Training for the peer listeners should include:

- listening skills

- reflection and paraphrasing skills

- questioning skills

- feedback

- role-plays

- scenarios

- confidentiality and child protection

You should also offer the peer listeners access to resources, ongoing supervision meetings and staff support.

Drop-in Sessions

It is advisable to have an accessible drop-in facility for all students when needed most – break and lunch times. A further idea is to run a lunchtime games club for vulnerable students who find such places as the dining hall or playground difficult.

Bullying Box

This facility can be used to alert staff about a bullying problem for those students too anxious to speak to someone face-to-face. Referral forms should be available with the box, alongside a poster clearly stating guidelines for making a referral.

Worksheets

On the following pages you will find some exercises that can be used with young people who might face bullying in the future. Like self-defence, this learning can restore damaged self-esteem and instill increased confidence about the future. However, they are not a substitute for staff action to stop the bullying if it is reported or observed.

Bullying Leaflet

This is a general introduction giving advice to students on how to deal with bullying. Discuss the leaflet with the student who can then keep it to refer to later.

Most People Have Experienced Bullying

The aim of this worksheet is to encourage the student to realise that he is not alone in his experience of bullying. The experience can encourage feelings of isolation and this sheet aims to discourage that emotion. It also enables the student to put his experience into words as once it is acknowledged, it can be easier to deal with. For those students who are displaying bullying behaviour, this sheet could encourage empathy and recognition of how students on the receiving end may be feeling.

We All Have the Right to Feel Safe

It is important that a person being bullied understands that it is through no fault of her own and that she, as everyone else does, has the right to feel safe. Young people sometimes find it difficult to disclose incidents of bullying and this sheet reinforces the importance of doing so, as it is the student's right to feel safe. It also helps the student to think of what makes her feel safe and recognise how to implement this in school. For use with a student who is bullying, the worksheet contemplates what feeling safe is and how her behaviour can violate or influence this.

My Support Circle

Being bullied can make a young person feel very alone. This sheet helps the pupil to identify whom she can ask for support. There are three circles. The inner circle closest to 'me' is where the student writes the names of those who are closest to her and can offer a lot of support. This could include family, or close friends, an adult she can talk to, and possibly yourself. The outer circle is for those in the community who could offer support, such as a doctor or counsellor. It is more interesting for the student to use lots of colour with this worksheet.

Ways to Cope with Bullying

Bullying can be a very distressing experience for young people. This list provides suggestions of different coping strategies for students to try. Talk through the options to ensure they understand any related issues, such as going for a walk when it is safe to do so – with a parent or when it is light (and with a parent/carer's permission).

Why Would Someone Bully?

This sheet attempts to help the targets of bullying understand why students bully, to make those people appear less threatening.

What I'd Say...

This sheet gives an opportunity for the student to express how he feels, whether he feels anger or confusion. This expression could be written, drawn or painted. It should provide insight into which issues need addressing.

Anti-bullying Plan of Action

This plan can be used to work both with students who are being bullied and students who are displaying bullying behaviour. It gives the student the responsibility to evaluate her progress in addressing the bullying, either as a perpetrator or a victim. It generates more specific actions for the student to try and offers the opportunity to re-focus the support and move forward. Part 1 allows for reflection and the student then writes the resulting action plan on Part 2. Evaluation of this takes place in Part 3, offering the chance to make changes if necessary.

Another idea is for the student to map out whom she will talk to about the bullying, with pathways of support if that person is not available or does not make a difference, thus covering all options.

Mediation

Some relationship disputes might arise between individuals or groups where anti-bullying strategies are not appropriate. Bullying is characterised by an imbalance of power where the target is powerless.

When both parties hold the power, this could be described as a 'conflict' or a 'dispute'. In these cases a procedure called mediation can be used and is seen as a fair and effective way to facilitate agreement between the disputants.

Guidance is provided on how to facilitate such mediation in order to resolve conflict; this does not always result in friendship but instead can allow the students to voice their opinions and agree the situation as settled in order to move forward.

Friends

Often young people do not realise how friends can influence them, in whichever form this may take. This worksheet has been created to be used with students who bully, but can also be used to help students who are being bullied recognise the effect friends may have on the situation, for example, supportive friends or those who may provoke the bullying.

Peer Pressure

This sheet gives the person demonstrating bullying behaviour the chance to analyse her friends' actions in terms of the influence it has on her. What friends do (that they try to get the student involved in) is written in the 'action' box. In the second box, the student writes the thoughts that she has that justify why she should join in. The third box asks the young person to think what alternative thoughts she could have that would lead to her deciding it would not be a good idea to join in.

Who are the Victims?

This sheet recognises the immediate and wider victims of bullying behaviour. Many instigators of bullying do not realise the full effect of their actions upon friends and family – both of the person being bullied and the person bullying. It should also be used to consider the concept of bullying and its consequences on the school and in society more generally.

Victim

This sheet encourages somebody who is victimising someone else to think about the effects of his behaviour. The names of the people being affected should be put in the first shape and then what they might think about the action is written in the thought bubble. Finally, the student has to imagine what the victim may feel about this behaviour in the round box that is outer most. This encourages empathy, giving students a tool to start to see things from another person's point of view.

Activities

Bullying Scenarios

This provides the opportunity to present bullying situations hypothetically so that students can consider solutions in the third-person. Young people often find it useful to contemplate situations when they are not personal. A student can think of different dimensions to the scenario and possible resolutions that can then be related to his own experience. The scenarios can be used with both perpetrators and those targeted by bullying. Create your own scenarios that may be more relevant to the student but that are still distinct from his own experience.

Circle Time – Bullying

This is a sample of how a small group could be run using Circle Time, dealing with bullying from the perspective of the person displaying bullying behaviour, but in a way that does not condemn him.

In a group like this, those accused of bullying behaviour (with some evidence supporting the accusation) could, by attending, challenge the policies of the school. This takes the emphasis away from discipline, and concentrates on investigating why students are in that position in the first place. It would also mean that revenge would be less likely for those wanting to report bullying behaviour.

Helpful Contacts and Further Reading

www.antibullying.net

www.bullying.co.uk

www.childline.org.uk/bullying.asp

www.kidscape.org.uk

www.scre.ac.uk/bully

Alexander, J. (2006) *Bullies, Bigmouths and So-called Friends*. London: Hodder Children's Books.

Elliott, M. (1998) *Wise Guides – Bullying*. London: Hodder Children's Books.

Robinson, G. and Maines, B. (1992) *The No Blame Approach*. Bristol: Lucky Duck Publishing.

Salter Hampson, K. (2008) *Setting Up And Running A Peer Listening Scheme*. Oxford: Routledge.

Bullying!

Q: What do these famous people have in common?

- Victoria Beckham
- Jennifer Ellison
- Tom Cruise
- Christina Aguilera
- Ben Stiller
- Whitney Houston
- Taylor Swift
- Patsy Palmer
- Harrison Ford (Indiana Jones!)
- Brian McFadden
- Chester Bennington (Linkin Park)
- Miley Cyrus

A: They were all bullied at school!

What can I do if I am being bullied?

- Always tell an adult that you trust, such as your parent/carer, your form tutor or a teacher. You need their help and support – don't keep it to yourself.

- Don't fight back if you can help it.

- Try to avoid being alone in places you know a bully is likely to pick on you.

- Stick with a group, even if they are not your friends.

- Tell an adult – you need their help. Don't keep it to yourself.

- Try some of the assertiveness techniques on the next page.

The Learning Mentor's Resource Book		
Student use	Chapter Seven: Bullying	
Photocopy or print from CD-ROM		

10-14

133

Self-assertiveness

If you are a victim of bullying you are probably being passive. This means you behave as if other people's rights matter more than yours. If you are a bully you are probably aggressive. This means you behave as if your own rights matter more than other people's.

If you are assertive you can stand up for yourself without hurting others. You respect yourself and others equally.

With practice you can change your behaviour so that you are assertive!

- **Thoughts:** If we put ourselves down
  and feel we are no good, others will start
  to think so too!

- **Making requests:**

  1. Be clear about what you want.
  2. Make your requests short.
  3. Plan and practise, so you are prepared. Repeat your request in the same way if it is ignored.

- **Saying 'No':**

  1. Decide what you are going to say and stick to it – be kind but firm.

  2. Keep your body assertive – walk tall, don't smile, make eye contact or look straight ahead.

  3. Practise looking people in the eye.

  4. When you say 'No', say it firmly.

  5. Don't get sidetracked into apologising.

  6. Try not to get caught up in arguments.

7. If you don't want to do something don't give in to pressure.

8. If you are not sure and someone is bugging you for an answer say: 'I need more time', or, 'I need more information.'

9. Offer an alternative to what they are suggesting.

- **Shouting 'NO':** This is different from saying it, and can be used if you are in danger or need help quickly. Make it sound like a foghorn, not high and squeaky!!

- **Dealing with taunts:** If we insult back when people insult us, things can get quickly out of control. We need to try something else. Fogging – imagine a fog around you that soaks up what people are saying to you. You can either say nothing in return, or say something short such as, 'That's what you think', or 'It's possible'.

- **Relaxing helps you think more clearly:**

  1. Lie on the floor.
  2. Tense all your muscles until really rigid.
  3. Slowly relax your muscles, working from your toes up.

Most people have experienced bullying

The Learning Mentor's Resource Book
Student use | Chapter Seven: Bullying
Photocopy or print from CD-ROM
10-14

Most People Have Experienced Bullying

Write an experience of being bullied that you have had or witnessed...

_____

_____

_____

_____

_____

_____

_____

_____

_____

What were your feelings?

_____

_____

_____

_____

_____

_____

_____

_____

_____

We All Have the Right to Feel Safe

What helps you feel safe in school?

_____

_____

_____

_____

_____

_____

_____

_____

What do you have to do to help others in school feel safe?

_____

_____

_____

_____

_____

_____

_____

_____

My Support Circle

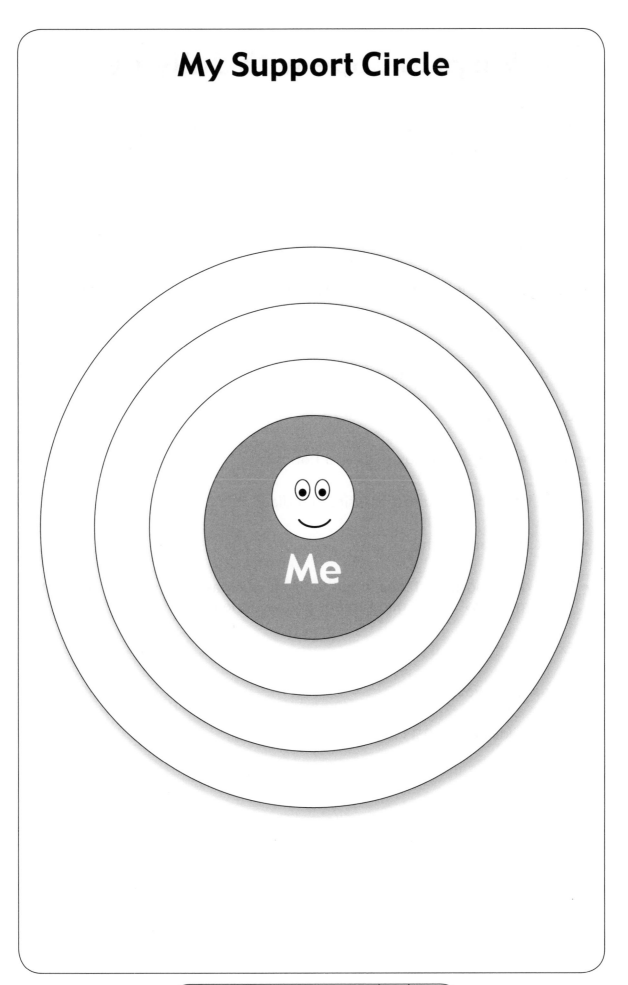

Me

Ways to Cope with Bullying

It is easy to let bullying worry you and get you down. Here are some ways you could try to help you cope...

- Talk to somebody in your Support Circle

- Go for a walk (if safe)

- Listen to your favourite music – something happy!

- Watch a good film

- Read a book or magazine

- Draw a picture

- Do something you enjoy such as a hobby

- Write down how you feel or write in a diary

- Relax in a warm bath

- Write down positive things about yourself, such as what you are good at, what you enjoy doing, good things you've done today

- Exercise

- Play a game you enjoy

- Ring ChildLine: 0800 1111

-

-

-

Why Would Someone Bully?

Young people bully others for many different reasons. Can you think of any reasons why someone is a bully?

_____
_____
_____
_____
_____
_____
_____
_____
_____
_____
_____
_____
_____
_____
_____
_____
_____
_____
_____
_____

Sometimes, children end up bullying others because they feel bad about themselves and try to cover it up. Some children think being a bully makes them look 'big'. Some children do not have many friends. Some children have problems outside of school that they cannot manage.

This doesn't mean that bullying is OK. Bullying is definitely not OK. But thinking of bullies in this way might make them seem less scary.

What I'd Say...

Use this sheet to write down exactly what you would like to say to the bully!
What would you like to ask them? Get your feelings out.

Anti-bullying Plan of Action

Part 1

Answer these questions:

1. Am I happy with the way things are going? If not, what can I do to change things?

> [ ]

2. Am I doing something to make myself or others unhappy? If so, it is my responsibility to change.

> [ ]

3. What can I do differently?

> [ ]

4. What will happen if I continue as I am? What choices do I have? Make a list. Which one thing can I work on today or this week?

> [ ]

5. a) What will I do when I see the person I am bullying?

> [ ]

   b) What will I do if I see the person who is bullying me?

> [ ]

6. Should I be changing anything that I am doing?

> [ ]

7. What will my goal be for the day, week, term, year?

> [ ]

Use the Plan of Action Part 2 to write down a point by point plan.

The Learning Mentor's Resource Book		
Student use	Chapter Seven: Bullying	10-14
Photocopy or print from CD-ROM		

141

Anti-bullying Plan of Action

Part 2

1.

2.

3.

4.

5.

6.

7.

8.

9.

10.

The Learning Mentor's Resource Book

Student use | Chapter Seven: Bullying

Photocopy or print from CD-ROM

10-14

Anti-bullying Plan of Action
Part 3

Use these questions to assess how the plan is working, and to change it if necessary.

1. How did I feel?

2. What else could I have done?

3. Did the action I took help the situation or make it worse?

4. What will I try next?

5. Can I name one thing that changed the situation for the better?

6. What did I learn about myself?

7. What is my goal now?

The Learning Mentor's Resource Book		
Student use	Chapter Seven: Bullying	10-14
Photocopy or print from CD-ROM		

143

Mediation

- Sometimes when friends argue, one of them ends up feeling bullied by the other, as feelings run high and things are said that could be regretted later on. This kind of situation is often best resolved with the provision of mediation between the two parties. The mediator should be someone who is neutral about the needs of both students.

- The key to mediation is providing uninterrupted time for each side to put their case forward, and ensuring each side listens to the other.

- When the students arrive at the session, try to ensure that they are sitting in such a way that they can see each other clearly but the mediator is sitting between them. Try to set out the chairs so the pupils are not directly opposite to each other.

- Lay down the ground rules before beginning, making sure that each student knows that the other student must not be interrupted. Explain that you will give each student the chance to speak and then to reflect upon what they feel about what the other pupil has said. After this you will identify the points that they agree upon, and build the solution based on those.

- Give the students the choice as to who wants to go first, and if both are reluctant, just choose!

- Give the first student a chance to say what the situation is from her own point of view, gently reminding the other student to wait if he tries to interrupt. Then turn to the other pupil, and give him chance to put forward his point of view. After both sides have done this, give each student time to give their view of what the other student has said (with no interruptions).

- Usually the feelings of each student surprise the other, and they find that they can proceed as friends from there. Sometimes this does not happen, but the two students can agree not to hurt each other anymore, and decide that they are best having different friends. This is not a failure, but a moving on to a (usually) less destructive acquaintance.

- The process can be repeated if one or other of the students is felt not to be keeping to the agreement.

Friends

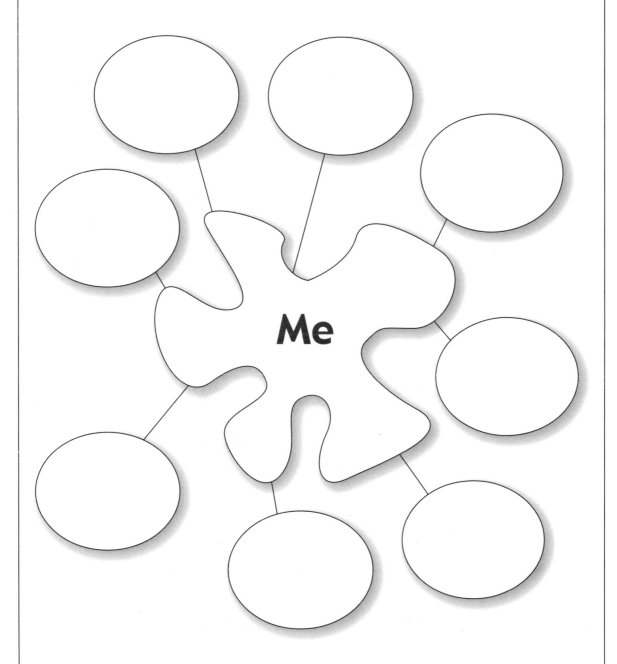

Colour the name of every friend as follows:

- Red if they influence you to do negative things.
- Yellow if they are neither a negative nor a positive influence.
- Green if they influence you to do positive things.

Peer Pressure

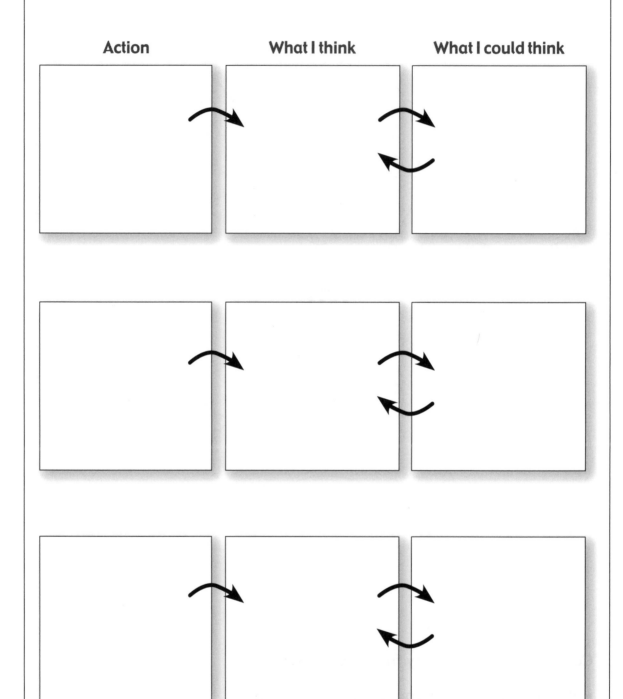

Action	What I think	What I could think

The Learning Mentor's Resource Book

Student use | Chapter Seven: Bullying

Photocopy or print from CD-ROM

10-14

Who are the Victims?

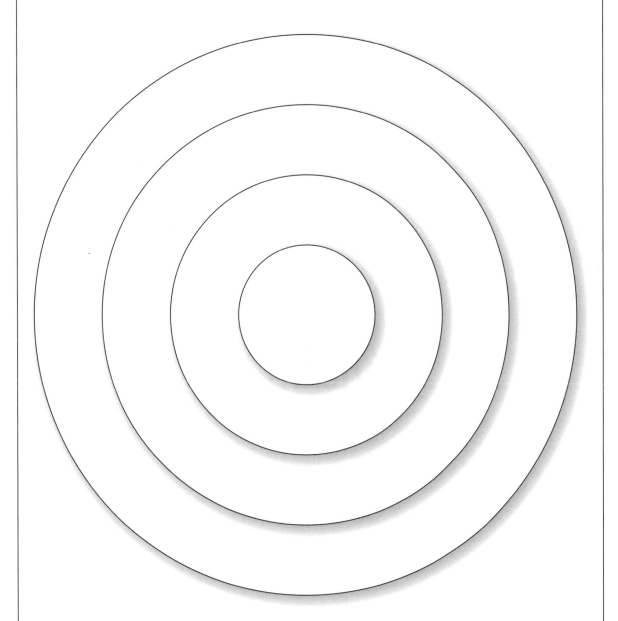

Who are the victims of your actions?

Think about everyone who has been affected in any way (whether you know them or not!)

Put the most affected in the more central circles and the less affected in the outer circles.

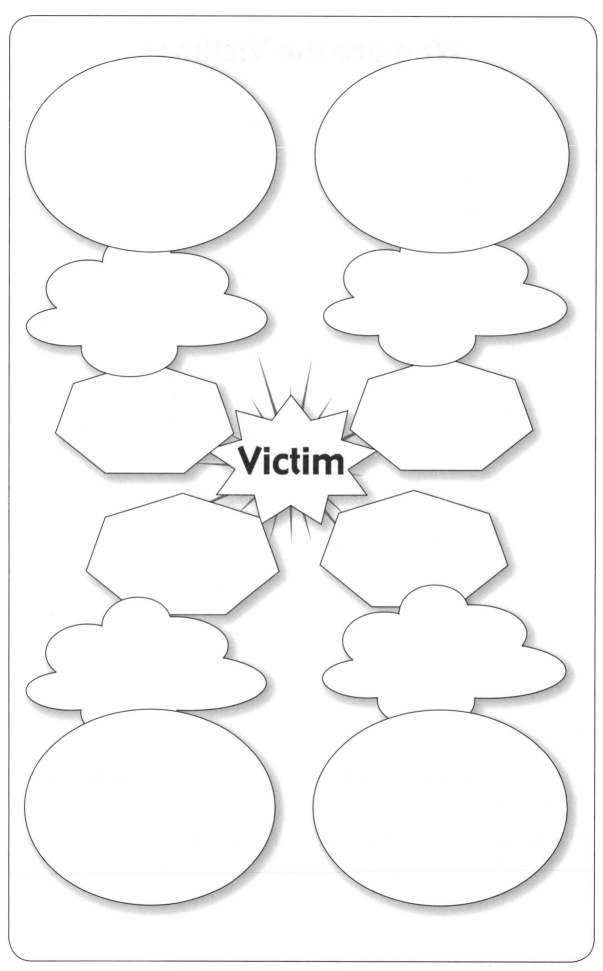

The Learning Mentor's Resource Book

Student use — Chapter Seven: Bullying

Photocopy or print from CD-ROM

10-14

Bullying Scenario 1

Sharon came to school new in Year 8, having moved house. She wears glasses, and has been called names since her first day. She has made some friends, but they have also been called names. They are starting to avoid her, hoping that the name-calling would stop. Sharon is now starting to say she feels sick in the mornings to avoid coming to school. Her mum is very worried about her.

What are the bullying issues?

_____

_____

_____

_____

Who is affected by the name-calling?

_____

_____

_____

_____

Who could have changed the situation?

_____

_____

_____

_____

What are the possible endings for the story?

_____

_____

_____

_____

Bullying Scenario 2

Robert is in Year 9. His dad is of white origin and his mum is Chinese. Robert has been getting called names about being half-Chinese for a while but he has been trying to ignore it. Recently, the boys who are calling him names have starting pushing him around and threatening to wait for him after school. Robert has started to lose his temper easily at home and is arguing more with his brother and parents.

What are the bullying issues?

_____
_____
_____
_____

Who is affected by the name-calling?

_____
_____
_____
_____

Who could have changed the situation?

_____
_____
_____
_____

What are the possible endings for the story?

_____
_____
_____
_____

Bullying Scenario 3

Emma is in Year 10 and finds reading difficult. She gets embarrassed about this in class so to hide this, she misbehaves. Emma thinks acting tough keeps her safe from others noticing her problems with reading and picking on her for that. There is another girl in her class who is good at schoolwork. She starts to throw things at this girl and trip her up in the dining hall. Emma gets her friend, Sunita, involved. Sunita does not really think it's nice to act like this but Emma keeps telling her to 'be a mate and just do it or we won't be friends'.

What are the bullying issues?

Who is affected by the name-calling?

Who could have changed the situation?

What are the possible endings for the story?

The Learning Mentor's Resource Book		
Student use	Chapter Seven: Bullying	10-14
Photocopy or print from CD-ROM		

151

Circle Time – Bullying

Activity	Details	What's needed
Introduction	Introduce the subject matter by explaining that the group will be looking at bullying: what it is, why people do it, and what feelings it causes. Ensure that the Circle Time 'rules' of being able to pass if need be, being able to say what someone else has already said if it's relevant, and keeping all contributions positive and non-personal (no names ever mentioned) are clear before the start.	
Icebreaker	All members of the group (facilitators included) introduce themselves to the rest of the group by saying their name and a pet they could have that begins with the same letter as their name (this could extend to tigers and donkeys!)	
What is bullying?	Using a speaking object, go round the circle completing the sentence: 'Bullying is...' (This could be done with a big piece of paper in the middle with contributions written in thick felt tips around a central sentence starter. This could be a less threatening way to begin.)	Speaking object Or Large paper and pens
Emotions (person being bullied)	Go through the Emotion Cards (See Chapter One), and decide as a group which emotions would be felt at some point by someone who has been bullied in the ways listed above. Put the relevant emotions in a separate pile, and then recap them afterwards. (This could also be done by dealing out the cards to each participant, and asking them to put theirs next to one of two signs saying 'yes' or 'no'.)	Emotion Cards A4 signs 'yes' 'no'
What makes someone bully someone else?	Same format as 'What is bullying?' exercise. Choose one of the methods (depending on how well the group are responding), and ask for endings to the sentence: 'What makes someone bully...?'	Speaking object Or Large paper and pens
Emotions (person bullying)	Same format as for 'Emotions' exercise above, this time considering what the person bullying would feel. If possible, use two sets of Emotion Cards (different colours?) and then compare the two piles of emotions afterwards (chances are there will be many similarities).	Emotion Cards A4 signs 'yes' 'no'

Bullying scenarios	Using the bullying scenarios in this chapter, in pairs with different scenarios, complete the exercise, then share the results with the whole group. Work out, as a whole group, a different outcome for each scenario. How could the actors have behaved differently?	Bullying scenarios Pens
What if I...?	One of the facilitators pretends to be someone who is being bullied in school. They say what is happening to them and how it makes them feel (use a pretend name, and act the part). Each member of the group, passing a speaking object, completes the sentence: 'Would it help if I...?'	Speaking object
Sentence completion round	Go round using a speaking object, with each group member (including facilitators) completing the sentence: 'I could help prevent bullying in school by...'	Speaking object
End round	Passing a speaking object round, change the introductory exercise, by this time each person introducing the person next to them, and saying a hobby they could do, beginning with the same letter as their name.	Speaking object

Chapter Eight
INTERNET SAFETY

Introduction

The internet is an amazing tool which brings the world into your home. Homework is made easier, research is more effective and comprehensive. However, because it gives access to *everything*, it is accompanied by risks and unsavoury material. Young people can now be groomed by strangers in their own homes, and pornography is universally available.

Many parents feel unable to cope technically with controlling their children's usage and so they trust internet filtering programmes, which are meant to screen out unsuitable material but in fact are easily circumvented by today's computer-savvy young people. It is important not to panic and throw the baby out with the bathwater. Young people's access to the internet is viewed as being so important that the UK government wants to pay for families who cannot afford it to be subscribed to broadband services. Most young people's typing speed is phenomenal, largely due to using instant messaging services in conversation with their friends. However, dangers are well documented in magazines and newspapers reporting incidences of young people being deceived by older adults pretending to be peers and gaining their trust, and persuading them to meet up in secret.

This section aims to provide materials for use both with young people, to help them to keep themselves safe, and with parents, to help them understand how they can monitor what their children do online.

Worksheets

Have You Ever?

This is a good introductory exercise to help you get some idea of what a young person might have been doing online. Simply ask the student to identify which of the online activities she has participated in, and then go through them using the 'Have you ever?' comments sheet which follows the worksheet. We would be inclined to go through the ones she has not ticked first asking her to say why she has not done them, to see if she is conscious of the dangers, before going through the ones she has done. You could ask her to identify emotions that went with the action (positive and negative). If you can get her to identify the dangers herself through a discussion she is more likely to take notice of them.

Internet Speak...for Beginners

This is a list of common internet terms which can be useful both for young people and their parents. For parents trying to keep up with what their children are doing online, this can be a useful resource to use as a leaflet, so it could be printed on A5 and given out to any parents who would like it.

Being Internet-wise...

This is a leaflet for all young people, providing basic common sense advice for any internet use. It could be printed on A5 (with the internet-speak on the back if desired) and given out to all pupils, or targeted pupils. It could also be printed as a poster and displayed at all internet access points around the school.

Being Internet-wise... for Parents

This is a single sheet offering advice for parents about keeping their children safe on the internet. It could be used well at a parents' event, providing a forum for parents to discuss this area in further detail and gain support from each other. Many parents are much less internet-savvy than their children, and may not know where to go for help and advice. Their children, conversely, may not want them to be well informed! If resources allow, it could be posted out to every parent of pupils in the school.

Internet Scenarios

These scenarios should be printed out and preferably laminated for use. They can be used as discussion starters within groups, or with individuals felt to be at particular risk of being exploited. Lead a discussion about a few chosen cards, helping the pupil to identify what the characters might feel, what the dangers might be, and what could happen next. Challenge their assumptions about the situations, for example, the fact that what people say might not be the truth, and that photos they send may not be of themselves.

In the News...

This is a selection of real news stories about a variety of internet-related incidences, each highlighting different dangers. You could use them in a very targeted way, discussing with pupils how the situation might have arisen, and how the young person involved could have prevented it by being more internet-wise. Clearly it is important not to blame the victim for becoming prey to a criminal on the internet, but the vital message is that there are lots of ways to keep yourself safe. The scenarios can be printed out as a worksheet, or cut into individual laminated cards, which are then used more selectively.

Instant Messages

This worksheet uses what could be an innocent instant message conversation between two young people, but equally could be something much more sinister. There are discussion questions on the sheet, but you need to remember to challenge a pupil's assumptions about what she is reading. You could set up two different profiles that could equally describe the 'Cute guy' character, one whom is largely as he writes, and one being someone significantly older, who consistently lied and sent someone else's photo. Ask the pupil to say which of these 'Cute guy' is, and why. Challenge, if necessary, what proof she will accept of someone's identity, and whether this could be falsified.

Useful contacts

www.noslang.com/dictionary

www.thinkuknow.co.uk/11_16/

www.ceop.gov.uk/

www.kidsmart.org.uk/

www.getnetwise.org/

http://www.getsafeonline.org/

Have You Ever?

Tick the box if you have ever done one of the following things (be honest!):

☐ Told someone you have never met, but talked to online, something personal about yourself

☐ Sent a picture of yourself to someone you have never met

☐ Told someone else a password

☐ Said something to someone online that you wouldn't say in real life

☐ Been worried by something someone has said or done to you online

☐ Posted a video on the internet

☐ Posted a photo of yourself somewhere on the internet

☐ Replied to a 'spam' email

☐ Clicked on a link in an email

☐ Opened an email attachment from someone you don't know

☐ Opened a picture from someone you don't know

☐ Met someone in real life you have got to know online

☐ Had someone say something nasty to you online

☐ Told someone online your home address

☐ Told someone online your date of birth

☐ Sent an email or message to someone when you were angry and regretted it later

☐ Clicked on a 'pop-up' and felt shocked by a picture that came up

☐ Accepted a 'friend' request on a networking site from someone you don't know

☐ Lied about yourself online

Have You Ever?

Use the following comments on the questions that were ticked to have a discussion about the risks that may have been opened up. Always gently ask what made the young person decide to do the action they ticked, not accepting any 'don't know' responses, as there will always be a reason (even if that reason is that they couldn't see any danger in it!)

☐ Told someone you have never met, but talked to online, something personal about yourself

Revealing personal information is risky because you don't know what the other person might use it for. You also do not know whether they are who they say they are!

☐ Sent a picture of yourself to someone you have never met

Similarly to the above, you don't know what someone will do with a photo of you. An alarming number of young people have been persuaded to send someone a picture of themselves with no, or few, clothes on, and in positions they are not comfortable about. However, there is still risk in simply letting someone else know what you look like, as they may then be able to make more direct contact with you. They may also have information about you that you haven't revealed to non-virtual friends or family.

☐ Told someone else a password

There is no reason why someone else should know any of your passwords. As soon as you reveal one to someone, you lose control of that information, as they can do what they like with it! You may think that it is OK to tell a friend, but always think what might happen if you fall out! Someone having access to a password means that they can access that application whenever they want, and do whatever they want with it.

☐ Said something to someone online that you wouldn't say in real life

*This can be very tempting, especially if you have a problem you can't discuss with anyone you know. However, **never forget** that there is a real person on the other end of your conversation who might not keep what you say to themselves, or might try to get information out of you that you wouldn't normally tell anyone. It's easy to think 'no one knows who I am online', but this is not always true!*

☐ Been worried by something someone has said or done to you online

Be aware that other people may well say things online that they wouldn't say in real life, and some of these things might be mean, rude, or disturbing in another way. People think that because the internet can make you feel anonymous, it doesn't matter what you say. When people commit crimes online, or confess to commiting a crime online, the police have ways of tracing them, so there is more accountability than people often think. However, this doesn't mean that people will always do what's right on the internet. Never be afraid to tell someone when you feel upset or worried about something that has happened online. Many websites also have ways you can report abusive behaviour. Use them!

☐ Posted a video on the internet

Always remember that anything you put on the internet becomes public property. You would be amazed how much something can be spread around on different websites, just from someone making one posting. If you do post a video on the internet, make sure you ask anyone who features in it whether they mind, and think about whether you would be worried if your friends, family, or strangers saw it. If it doubt, don't do it!

☐ Posted a photo of yourself somewhere on the internet

This is similar to the video posting, except that photos are much more easily obtained, and therefore much more likely to be put on the internet in quantity. If you put photos of yourself on a networking site, see if you can set your preferences to make it impossible for someone to 'steal' your photos, and even better, only allow your profile to be seen by your 'real' friends!

☐ Replied to a 'spam' email

'Spam' is email which has been sent to you by people or companies you don't know and you haven't asked for. It can open up undesirable sites like those including pornography, and can let someone know that the email address they contacted is a 'live' one (the chances are they sent hundreds of emails out to email addresses in the hope that some will be opened, showing that someone will respond). The only way to give the impression that your email address is not real is by deleting the email without reading it first!

☐ Clicked on a link in an email

*Many 'spam' emails include bogus email links which help them to get hold of information like passwords, which they will then use without you even knowing. It is extremely difficult to see whether the site the link has led you to is genuine, because they are very well copied! You may not know until someone uses a piece of information which you typed into a bogus website that you were scammed in this way. This is very common for bank spam, which try to get passwords for bank accounts. As a result of this, all banks give the advice NEVER to click on a link in an email which is apparently from them. *Hint: the letters or words immediately before the .com (or whatever one it happens to be) give you the best clue as to what any website really is. The words or letters which start it, or are put before a dot tell you nothing, as they can be made up!**

☐ Opened an email attachment from someone you don't know

Many viruses are spread through unsolicited emails from contacts you don't know, so the best advice is never to open an attachment like this. However, sometimes viruses are spread by someone getting into the address book of people and sending infected emails to all their contacts. This is much more difficult to spot before opening. You can safeguard yourself against this by adding a false email to the beginning of your address book, which cannot possibly be genuine (e.g. aaa@aaa.com), which would then send you a failed email delivery notice if your account sent an email to it, alerting you to the fact that an email had been sent without your knowledge.

☐ Opened a picture from someone you don't know

Some people send pictures on the internet to anyone who doesn't take enough care that will shock, hurt or otherwise upset. The only way to make sure that this cannot happen is to have a rule for yourself only to open pictures from people in your address book. This also minimises the chances of receiving a virus in this way.

☐ Met someone in real life you have got to know online

You can NEVER know whether someone online has been telling you the truth. They may say that they are a 14-year-old girl, but how do you know they are not really a 43-year-old man? It is a mistake to think that you know someone when you have been chatting on the internet. In reality you only know what they have told you, and what you want to hear! It may be uncomfortable to accept that people are not always what they seem. If you agree to meet someone, in reality, you have no idea who you are really meeting. They may have sent you a picture of someone else saying it is them, but if you have sent them a picture of you, they will recognise you before you know what has happened. This is NEVER a safe thing to do, but it can be made even more risky by meeting someone and not telling anyone what you are doing.

☐ Had someone say something nasty to you online

The internet is used by people who want to bully others, like other things are. It is easier to bully on the internet, as they don't have to actually face their victim. Never accept someone's abuse of you, block them if you can, and always tell someone about it, which will help you to deal with it better.

☐ Told someone online your home address

As previously discussed, people online are not always what you think they are, so you do not know who you are really giving your address to. It also allows someone to steal your identity, and possibly run up debts or other bills in your name.

☐ Told someone online your date of birth

Although it seems like a small thing, knowing someone's date of birth also allows them to steal your identity. This is often used in different accounts to set up or get access, so keep this piece of information to yourself! (Be careful if you put it on a networking site, especially if you cannot control who can look at this.)

☐ Sent an email or message to someone when you were angry and regretted it later

Sending a message or an email is a very instant thing to do – leaving no time to think about what is wise and what is not! Friendships can be ruined by responding too quickly and, more seriously, can have other consequences, like police action, as they are recorded and can be kept.

The Learning Mentor's Resource Book		
Facilitator use	Chapter Eight: Internet Safety	11-16
Photocopy or print from CD-ROM		

159

☐ Clicked on a 'pop-up' and felt shocked by a picture that came up

When browsing the internet, boxes sometimes pop up on the screen (hence the name!), which may include a picture and a link to a website. These are often adverts, sometimes pornography or gambling sites. Once clicked, the site knows there is interest, and this can lead to much more unsolicited material of this type. The best advice is always to click on the 'x' in the corner, never to click on 'close' if this is an option. Clicking on any part of the pop up will usually take the user to the site, even if they clicked on 'close'!

☐ Accepted a 'friend' request on a networking site from someone you don't know

Remember, you do not know who this person is, and therefore they could be anyone! You may think that anyone who wants to be your friend must be alright, but you do not know why they are requesting this. If they are not who they say they are (and are in fact a 43-year-old man instead of a 14-year-old girl, for example), they may be 'grooming' with a view to having an unsuitable or even illegal relationship with you. Grooming is when someone is very persuasive and becomes your friend for a reason that is not nice. There have now been many convictions of people attempting to dupe young people into underage sexual relationships with them by using the internet in this way. Also, if you feel that there can't possibly be any harm in simply accepting someone as a friend, this might give them access to information about you that they would not otherwise get. They might use this information to pretend to be someone you would be interested in.

☐ Lied about yourself online

If you have ever lied abut yourself online, and I bet you have, remember that this is also true of the millions of other people online...and you don't know what they might be lying about. It might be trivial, but it might be completely mind-blowing in its deception!

Internet Speak... for Beginners

- Avatar – a character which represents a user online
- Blog – an online diary usually written by an individual
- Bookmark – an online marker for a particular website you might want to revisit (also called a 'favourite')
- Cookie – a piece of information sent from a website to a web browser (computer), which is then stored
- Emoticon – a text-based face to give internet users the opportunity to express emotion in online communications (e.g. :-) = smiley face)
- FAQ – frequently asked questions
- GIF – (Graphic Interchange Format) a picture format
- Hyperlink – a word you can click on to take you to another web page
- IP address – a code of numbers which identifies every computer on the internet
- ISP – internet service provider
- JPEG – (Joint Photographic Experts Group) another picture format
- PDF – (Portable Document Format) type of document format
- Phishing – emails which try to gain personal information fraudulently by pretending to be from banks etc, asking for passwords and other information
- Podcast – audio online broadcast
- Pop-up advert – an advert which suddenly appears in a new browser window on your screen. Pop-up blockers can stop this occurring
- Post – a comment made on a website by the user
- Social networking sites – these are websites which allow people to put up a profile and contact others online. The profiles have as much or as little information as the user wants to include, and can usually be set to be viewed by restricted ranges of people. This is wise to reduce grooming and identity theft opportunities
- Spam – email sent to a large number of recipients who didn't ask for it
- Streaming – a way of listening to or watching media files without fully downloading them first. They are not generally stored on your computer
- Trojan – a programme which masquerades as something else to trick the user into running it
- Virus – a computer code that can replicate itself without any human intervention. Often refers to damaging programmes sent maliciously to destroy people's computers without detection
- Webmaster – person in charge of administering a website
- Web ring – a way of visiting other similar websites (by clicking on a web ring hyperlink)
- Wi-Fi – (Wireless Fidelity) wireless computer networking
- Wiki – a website which allows users to easily edit it

The Learning Mentor's Resource Book
Student and Facilitator use | Chapter Eight: Internet Safety | 13-16
Photocopy or print from CD-ROM

161

Being Internet-wise...

- Don't tell people your personal information – you don't know what they might do with it!

- Never send pictures of yourself to strangers – keep them for your friends!

- Always keep your passwords secret.

- Don't do anything online that you wouldn't do offline.

- Always keep your profiles limited to friends-only access.

- Only add people as 'friends' who you know in real life.

- Don't open files or attachments from people you don't know.

- NEVER meet up with someone you only know from the internet – they may not be who they say they are!

- Remember that anyone can see what you put online. This includes photos and videos.

- Don't reply to spam or junk email – you will just make it worse!

- Tell a trusted adult if something happens that worries, scares, or upsets you.

The Learning Mentor's Resource Book

Student use | Chapter Eight: Internet Safety

Photocopy or print from CD-ROM

13-16

Being Internet-wise... for Parents

Keep internet access within family spaces. This way it is easier to keep an eye on what your children are doing online, and they know that anyone could just walk in! Familiarise yourself with net and text code (see http://www.noslang.com/dictionary).

Enable software which will not allow users access to certain types of sites you might find unacceptable. Most of these programmes allow you to set the level of access, but beware...the most computer-savvy young people can often get around these! But they are still good for younger children.

Learn how to be a computer-usage detective! Records of web pages that have been accessed are stored on your computer's hard drive. These differ from computer to computer, but will usually be stored in folders called 'cookies', 'temporary internet files' or 'history'. This record can be cleared at the stroke of a key, so make sure this hasn't been done before you can check! (A completely empty folder should be a warning that this record has been cleared...find out why!).

Do not allow your children to have their own password protected areas. This makes it very difficult to monitor what they are doing. If you pay the bill then you can choose how it is used!

Establish rules for internet usage as early as you can. This can include types of sites that are acceptable (and those that aren't!), time limits (young people would be on the internet all night if no one stopped them!), and sharing protocols. These rules could be made into a poster displayed above the points of access as a reminder.

If you start getting frequent 'pops-ups' from pornography sites, this may indicate that sites like that have identified that your computer has been used before to access such material. This is only a guide, and should prompt you to be more vigilant about what is being done, rather than proof, as pop-ups can be received randomly (but not usually in quantity).

Make sure your children have their social networking profiles set to 'friends only' so people they don't know cannot access their information. Try to be online 'friends' with your children, then you can see what's happening!

Advise your children never to do anything online they wouldn't do offline, and be alert to any changes in their behaviour which could indicate that something worrying is happening. Keep the channels of communication open so they will be able to talk to you should anything happen that worries or scares them.

The Learning Mentor's Resource Book
Facilitator/parent use | Chapter Eight: Internet Safety | ! | 13-16 | **163**
Photocopy or print from CD-ROM

Internet Scenarios

Your friend starts texting someone of the opposite sex who they got to know on the internet.	You and your friend are chatting to someone on the internet who asks for some photos of you.
You and your friend are chatting to someone on the internet who suddenly sends you a photo of themselves in just their underwear.	You and your friend are chatting to someone on the internet who suddenly sends you a photo of themselves in the nude.
Your friend tells you that someone they have been chatting to on the internet asked them to send a 'sexy' photo.	Your friend tells you that they have sent a photo of themselves in just their underwear to someone on the internet, because they were asked for it.
You are chatting to someone on the internet who you have got to know over the last few weeks, and they ask you to meet up with them.	You are chatting to someone on the internet who you have got to know over the last few weeks, and they ask you to send them a 'sexy' photo of yourself.

You are bombarded with abusive messages on the internet by someone who you refused to meet.	Someone who lives near you, but who you have never met, starts sending you threats through a networking site.
Someone you used to be friends with, until you fell out, starts posting lots of nasty comments about you on your main networking sites.	You have got to know someone through a chat room who is your age, and who you really fancy. They seem really nice, and ask you out on a date.
Someone has got into your networking site account and sent lots of abusive messages to all your friends.	Your friend tells you that they are going out on a date with someone they met on the internet, but swear you to secrecy.
Someone puts a mobile phone video on the internet of you when you were doing something really embarrassing.	An ex-boyfriend/girlfriend who you had an awful break-up with put a photo of you in your underwear on the internet along with a nasty caption.
Your friend asks you to cover for them while they meet someone they got to know on the internet, so they don't have to tell anyone.	Someone you have been chatting to on the internet for a few weeks starts making sexual comments to you.

In the News...

July 2009 – a 25-year-old man was found guilty of 'grooming' and several counts of 'sexual activity with a child', when he befriended girls as young as 13 on a networking site. He always pretended to be younger, knew the ages of the girls he contacted, and persuaded them to meet up and have sexual contact with him.

January 2008 – a man pleaded guilty of internet 'grooming' and was found with 200 indecent photos of girls aged 13 to 15 on his computer. He persuaded them to send him the images taken on mobile phones and webcams by promises of phone top-ups.

October 2007 – a 37-year-old man was jailed for internet grooming when he persuaded a 12-year-old girl to do a 'rude dare' for money. He pretended to be a 14-year-old girl, and obtained the victim's mobile number, sending increasingly explicit text messages. He was caught because his victim was actually an undercover police officer.

A 14-year-old girl was targeted by a 24-year-old man who claimed to be 15. She realised he had lied when he sent her a webcam link on which he exposed himself and performed an indecent act. She didn't tell anyone, and became increasingly depressed, self-harming to help herself feel better.

After she had eventually told someone, she advised: 'I would tell anyone to be open about anything on the internet that you don't feel comfortable with. I wish I had confided in my mum and dad.'

A 12-year-old girl was abducted from their holiday villa by a man she had previously met on a networking site. He had pretended to be 28, but was actually 41. He lured her from her villa, but abandoned her at the airport when he realised she did not have a passport with her.

June 2006 – a 14-year-old girl had sex with a 39-year-old man, after they had made contact through a teen networking site which was used by his children. He didn't lie about his age, but persuaded her to swap email addresses and mobile phone numbers, before arranging to meet up. They met several times during which they had sex. He was jailed for 30 months.

May 2009 – a 47-year-old man pretended to be a 19-year-old boy. He met a 14-year-old girl in a chat room, admitted his age after expressing his love for her, and arranged to pick her up. He took her to a bed and breakfast, where they had sexual contact, until the B & B owner grew suspicious and called the police. The police found indecent images of the girl and others of a similar age on his mobile phone and computer.

October 2009 – a 32-year-old registered sex offender was charged with killing a 17-year-old girl he met on a social networking site, after posing as a 16-year-old boy. The girl had told her mum she was staying overnight at a friend's house, but admitted to friends that she had a secret date with a 16-year-old she had met on the internet. Her body was discovered in a ditch.

A 64-year-old man befriended 73 teenage girls over 5 months through internet chat rooms, often by posing as a teenage boy. Some of the girls were as young as 12. He bombarded them with explicit texts and messages, and tried to lure 2 of them into his car. He plagued them with threatening messages and phone calls if they tried to stop contact.

Instant Messages

Cute guy: Hi there!

Happy girl: Hi!

Cute guy: a/s/l?

Happy girl: 14 yrs, girl, Lexboro' u?

Cute guy: 15, boy, Lex also!

Happy girl: u like it here?

Cute guy: 's ok i guess. U?

Happy girl: yeh ok. Not much to do at w/e tho

Cute guy: no wat u mean. u wanna go out n do something?

Happy girl: hmm dunno. Don't know u enuf yt

Cute guy: you wanna pic?

Happy girl: k

------------------sending file--------------------------------------

Cute guy: u get it?

Happy girl: yeh. Nt bad!

Cute guy: u got 1 ov u?

Happy girl: yeh

Cute guy: u send 2 me?

Happy girl: k

------------------sending file--------------------------------------

Cute guy: verrry nice! u pretty

Happy girl: thanks

Cute guy: so where d'u go?

Happy girl: what do u mean?

Cute guy: I mean in Lex..where u go on sats?

Happy girl: um well I go to the skate park. Hang there mostly wiv mates

Cute guy: u goin tomoz?

Happy girl: yeh might do. If it don't rain or something

Cute guy: might catch u there. Bin there sum sats. Ill look out 4 u

Happy girl: um k

------------------happy girl has signed out--------------------

- What has Happy girl found out about Cute guy?
- How can she know whether these things are true?
- What has Cute guy found out about Happy girl?
- How long do you think it took Cute guy to find out all this information?
- Who was leading the conversation?
- How do you think Happy girl feels now?
- What dangers do you think Happy girl has opened herself up to?
- Do you think she reaslises?
- What might happen next?

Chapter Nine
HATE BEHAVIOUR

Introduction

There are growing concerns within the UK and more globally that hate crimes are increasing. Hate incidents are described as those motivated by prejudice or hostility towards an individual, group or community, based upon the victim's race, disability, sexual orientation, gender or religion and beliefs (Home Office, 2009). A hate crime is a criminal offence motivated by the same. The spectrum of hate behaviour ranges from abuse and harassment to violent extremism, and while some people may experience such incidents in isolation, for others these are daily torments. Clearly, hate-motivated behaviour is a threat to community cohesion and personal wellbeing. Thus, the government have created a plan to tackle hate crime, placing a duty upon public sector services to consider how they can foster good relations between different communities to promote cohesion and help prevent hate incidents. In 2008, Ofsted began to inspect schools with regard to meeting their duty to promote community cohesion (Home Office, 2009). Staff need to be aware of school policy and strategies to deal with the perpetrators of hate behaviour and also of ways in which to support the victims.

Hate behaviour is different to bullying as it reflects more deeply-embedded and discriminatory beliefs. Although these beliefs are usually associated with adulthood, the roots are often in the attitudes and experiences heard and felt in childhood, and some adolescents and young children do present with discriminatory, hate-based views. It makes sense then to address behaviour presenting as hate-based as early as possible. We would suggest that simply implementing a punishment or consequence for the perpetrators will not serve to address the underlying attitudes. Dealing with hate behaviour requires one-to-one work using the suggested worksheets and activities below to explore issues of identity and the effects of hate behaviour upon individuals, groups and communities. Additionally, contact with the parents/carers of both parties is advisable to discuss the actions taken within school and communicate what will happen if the hate behaviour continues. This is particularly important for young people who may witness such attitudes within their home environment. If the behaviour constitutes a criminal offence then your local government website should contain information of the hate crime report centres in your vicinity, where such crimes can be reported anonymously should the student wish to take this action.

Schools have a responsibility to promote social awareness and cohesion, within both the curriculum and group work in non-academic periods, as part of a wider preventative approach. Certain education departments may find that their local government runs safer community projects that can support such an approach. For schools within communities where significant hostility exists between different community groups or towards a certain group, the school may wish to take a whole school, marketing-type approach to promote acceptance and cohesion, integrating this into a variety of lessons and assemblies.

When thinking about hate behaviour and identity, it is important to generate awareness of the complex interactions and combinations of identity; so termed 'intersectionality' in the governmental paper which cites findings from a Stonewall survey that black minority and ethnic lesbian and gay people are twice as likely to have experienced a physical assault as the average for non-BME lesbian and gay people (2009).

A word of caution with all the activities suggested below: in keeping with the ethos of mentoring, the child will benefit more from being subtly lead into considering a different viewpoint and the exercises are designed to help do this. However, this is a particularly emotive issue and overt views should be clearly challenged, although in a sensitive manner. The worksheets are flexible so it may be useful to think about the young person you are working with and adapt the exercises to suit the situation. Some activities will also work in a whole class environment and may fit into PHSCE or a similar lesson.

Worksheets

Our Country to an Alien

This worksheet may be more suitable for younger children or those young people whose discriminatory views seem to be newly-emerging, or who are becoming embroiled with individuals with more embedded beliefs. It may not be appropriate for a young person who is known to express more extreme views. It aims to encourage the child to think about and celebrate the difference and diversity within their own country, how they can impact on this and where various traditions may have come from.

My Perfect Community

This worksheet can be used for students who do hold some non-discriminatory views to highlight the value of diversity and cohesion in a community. With some guided conversation about their perfect community, this worksheet intends to help the student to appreciate any similarities to their own community.

Sense of Belonging

This worksheet is similar to the What Do We See exercise. It explores how people can choose to conform (or not) in a physical and non-physical way and raises discussion about individuality and belonging.

Impact on Victims

Try encouraging the young person to generate their own ideas of how hate behaviour can impact upon victims and then maybe use this sheet as a talking point or prompt sheet.

Personal Crest

Another exercise aimed at exploring identity. Explore the meaning of the pupil's surname using the internet or books from the library and design a crest to represent this using the worksheet in Chapter Ten. If in a group, share the crests afterwards to celebrate differences.

Activities

Use of Language

Create two headers of 'OK' and 'not OK' or similar and explore what words and language around diversity and difference are currently acceptable. You may need to conduct some prior research into this. This may be used as an exercise to challenge improper use of language by asking questions such as 'who would be hurt by this word?' or 'what does it suggest about the person?'. You could follow this with any of activities that explore how it feels to be different such the Identity Collage, drama or DVD discussions.

Identity Collages

Use a variety of media such as magazines, paint, fabrics and photographs to create a collage representing the young person's identity. A mixture of materials is encouraged to help demonstrate the many different components that make each of us an individual. It may help to encourage the student to think about different aspects of their personality and lives: what has inspired these characteristics, where do they come from, where do they live, what are their beliefs and their hobbies. It may be appropriate to complete a second collage to show how they think other people view them.

If a person has been the perpetrator of hate behaviour, within a safe, one-to-one environment over a number of sessions, ask them to make a collage about the individual or group that they have expressed discriminatory views about and use this as a tool to explore what their views are based on. Following this, a fourth picture could be created to represent how that individual or group may see themselves – it may be helpful to spend some sessions exploring the issue if it is a particular religion, for example. Finally, compare all four pictures for similarities and differences and discuss what it would be like if all four images were exactly the same. An additional activity could be to use the Emotion Cards in Chapter One to explore how they feel about how they are represented and how the discriminated 'group' may feel about how they have been depicted.

Community 'Snapshots'

Arrange to take the pupil out into their own community and take photos and collect items that represent the area. Make these into a collage or sculpture. This can be as big or small a project as you wish – encourage it to show the many different aspects often found in one community.

Learn, Learn, Learn!

Research any areas of difference that might glean interest in the young person, for example, a historical group like a Native American tribe, a different type of music, a disability issue or even a current affair. Watch TV programmes, explore the internet together, read books and magazines. Think about: what are the benefits to being different, what may be the disadvantages and what pressures do mainstream societies add. This activity can be used with either a victim or perpetrator and it may be useful to compare this to how the young person feels about themselves.

What Do We See

Ask the young person or group to describe what they see when they look at you or at look a picture of somebody famous or otherwise. This should highlight a physical description including skin colour and things like wearing glasses; ask the young person what this tells them about that person? Glasses may suggest an eyesight issue or wearing a cross or Star of David may indicate a religious belief, or not, as the case may be. Then ask what the person cannot see. This should elicit answers around a person's thoughts, beliefs, past experiences, family, intelligence, feelings, certain abilities and disabilities.

If running this in a group situation, stand the facilitator in the middle of a circle and ask people from different angles to describe only what they can see on you without moving from that spot i.e. one person may be able to see an arm and one ear but no eyes and another may see one eye and one ear. This exercise highlights different perspectives and the importance of learning about the whole picture. You could do this individually with a pupil by asking them to move around you in a circular fashion, describing what they see at each step.

Music and Meaning

Identify recent or well-known music from different cultural influences or which refer to different lifestyles. Play the songs for the young person and ask about what may have influenced the music or lyrics. You could also listen to music that may be a fusion of different cultural influences and explore this.

Being Different exercises

Explore how it feels to be a minority or to be disliked or even hated for something you can't change about yourself i.e. skin colour, sexuality, disability – something 'natural' about yourself. As a talking point only, you could visit www.janeelliott.com Following the assassination of Martin Luther King in 1968, Jane Elliott devised the controversial 'Blue Eyes/Brown Eyes' exercise in which an inferior or superior status was given based solely on eye colour. The inferior blue eyed people were then subjected to 'pseudo-scientific explanations of their inferiority, culturally-biased IQ tests and blatant discrimination'. While repeating these exercises is not recommended, you could explore how the people in such experiments felt using the Emotion Cards in Chapter One to help. Alternatively, you could read sections of a novel with the young person or a class if you are aware of a suitable one that explores this topic. For example, *The War between the Classes* by Gloria Miklowitz tells the story of a relationship between a boy and girl from different racial and social backgrounds who fight against prejudice from both parents and friends. A teacher at their school conducts a 'Colour Game', with similarities to the 'Blue Eyes/Brown Eyes' experiment.

Alternatively, and where appropriate with regard to levels of self-esteem and self-awareness, take the young person who may be a perpetrator of hate behaviour to a shopping mall or supermarket and hire a wheelchair whilst there or even invite them to wear an unusual and noticeable hat. The idea is to help them experience how an everyday activity such as this feels for someone who is made to feel different. It is important to explore these feelings afterwards and debrief. If the young person refuses, explore why with questions such as what is stopping them and what emotions are invoked.

Explore through Drama

Drama can provide the safety of a third person view point to explore themes that can seem sensitive or delicate to discuss such as diversity and the effects of hate behaviour. You could adapt scenes from existing plays or novels (such as *West Side Story* or *Romeo and Juliet*) or invite a drama company in to perform and participate in a workshop afterwards. There are a number of Theatre in Education companies and you could find out if there is one locally by contacting your local theatre, arts centre or education department. Your local council or arts council office may also hold this information. Local theatres often run themed workshops. Other activities could include freezing the scene and asking the audience to think of questions for the characters or writing how each character must be feeling on a flip chart.

DVD discussions

Show parts of a film or documentary and follow with discussions, or a workshop similar to the above, around the thoughts and feelings of the characters involved or social implications. Explore how the scene could be changed or alternative endings and their consequences. Examples of films that could be used are *Crash*, which explores different prejudices and is certified 15, or *Mississippi Burning* (rated 18) which could initiate a discussion about how unjust discrimination is. You must identify what scenes are appropriate and gain consent from parents due to the age certificates.

Get Out and About

Again with careful consideration of the young person, one idea is to visit predominantly ethnic minority communities in the local area and explore different products or foods, visit a restaurant or café and meet some of the local people. You may wish to make this a more formally arranged trip to check that people in the community are happy to talk about their experiences. Alternatively, through community relation groups, arrange for a representative to come into school and talk to a group of students about how it feels to belong to a certain group and live in this country, or how it feels to live with a certain disability.

Helpful Contacts and Further Reading

www.stophateuk.org Stop Hate UK

www.adl.org/prejudice/default.asp

Miklowitz, G. (1986) *The War between the Classes*. New York: Random House. See www.random house.com

Stern-LaRosa, C. and Hofheimer Bettmann, E. (2000) *Hate Hurts: How Children Learn and Unlearn Prejudice*. New York: Scholastic Inc. See www.adl.org/ctboh/hate_hurts

Our Country to an Alien

The country I live in is called ....

Write or draw what our country looks, sounds and smells like...

If I didn't live here, I would want to live in .... because..........................
....

5 good things about our country...

3 reasons why an Alien might want to live here...

3 things I didn't know about my country...

The Learning Mentor's Resource Book

Student use | Chapter Nine: Hate Behaviour

Photocopy or print from CD-ROM

10-16

My Perfect Community would be named...

Draw or write about...

What it looks like...

Who lives here....

What sort of things happen everyday...

What rules, law or systems would it have?

How would people know what the rules are? Who would make sure they are followed? What would happen if people did not do this?

....
....
....

How would your community change and grow?

How would your community survive? What would keep it going?

- How is your idea of a perfect community affected by your own past and experiences?
- What are the effects of history, both good and bad?
- What would need to be added to our own community to make it more like your perfect one?

Sense of Belonging

Dogs like company, cats like independence. What about humans?

People, especially teenagers, like to feel as though they belong somewhere, that they are accepted and liked. Growing up during your teenage years may see you have a push and pull relationship with your family and friends, where you try to do more of the behaviours you like in them or have been used to for all of your life while also trying hard to be your own person. Have you done something you know your parents would not like? (Just think this in your head!)

What groups do you belong to?

....
....
....

Are there any groups you don't belong do?

....
....
....

Are there any you would you like to part of?

....

Which are you pleased that you are not part of? ....

People can choose to show their identity, for example, through fashion or dress. How might you tell if someone is part of the following 'groups'?

Guides   Army Cadets   Punk   A football supporter

Think About...

Are there any trends in your school right now that lots of students are wearing or doing, such as the way you wear your tie or friendship bracelets?
Do you think they are trying to be individual or part of a 'group'?

People's identity and beliefs are not always visible. How can you tell by looking at someone if they are...

                    Religious   Healthy

Musical

        Homophobic   Trustworthy   Single

            Intelligent   Honest

    Political   Arty   Racist

Impact on Victims

- Anger and bitterness towards others

- Fear of repeat attacks

- Emotionally drained or damaged

- Worsening of existing mental or physical health conditions

- New health conditions such as depression

- Financial cost of repairing property or cost of income if absent from work or need to move house

- Change of appearance

- Change of routines like travel to school

- Avoid school or work and miss out on education and the social side

- Stay in the house more

- Fight back and get in trouble

- Change school, have to make new friends

- Poor self image

- Reinforces negative messages that may already exist in society – for example, wheelchair users are never in fairytales

The Learning Mentor's Resource Book		
Student use	Chapter Nine: Hate Behaviour	
Photocopy or print from CD-ROM		

11-16

175

Chapter Ten
BEHAVIOUR CHANGE

Introduction

Behaviour is an area of growing concern for teachers, parents, teaching unions, and some young people themselves. So much is said in the media about the falling standards of the behaviour of young people in schools (and more generally!) that in 2009 the Secretary of State issued the 'Behaviour Challenge' stating that a 'satisfactory' mark by Ofsted for behaviour was not good enough (Home Office, 2009). Within education, inclusion has become a buzzword quoted as an ideal for all schools to achieve, which may mean that some young people remain in mainstream schools who previously may have been sent to an alternative provision. This creates an extra challenge for those hoping to retain these students in education.

In the majority of cases of behaviour problems in school, the young person is usually demonstrating similar difficulties at home and parents may be just as concerned or struggling to manage certain behaviours. Therefore, the most effective approach in dealing with misbehaviour in school is to involve and communicate with the family. There has been an increase in support for parenting recently through Family Intervention Projects and parenting support programmes so staff may be able to signpost parents to extended or external services.

Often, medical explanations such as Attention Deficit Hyperactivity Disorder or Autistic Spectrum Conditions are sought for behaviour problems. ADHD is often perceived purely as *hyper*activity but the behaviours displayed in ADHD children fall into the categories of inattention, impulsivity and overactivity. Seeking a diagnosis can be a 'red herring' as most children will not have any such condition. It is important to remember that they apply only to a very small minority. If parents or staff still believe there is an underlying issue, advice can be sought from the family GP who can refer to local, more specialist Children and Adolescent Mental Health Services (CAMHS) for a full assessment. It is worth noting that while any assessment is being applied for, behaviour management techniques should still be put in place, particularly as this often makes up part of the package of care following a diagnosis – after all, the behaviour will still exist! Furthermore, if parents or staff become 'fixated' on the possibility of a diagnosis this can be unhelpful as the child may internalise the message that they are 'hyper' or something is 'wrong'. For the small number of children who are diagnosed, there are services available such as CAMHS who can offer consultation regarding the management of the behaviour plus a wide choice of useful literature for parents, teaching staff and support workers.

Nevertheless, the behaviour materials in this chapter are a starting point for anyone embarking on individual behaviour work with a young person, with or without parental involvement or a diagnosis. It is helpful to identify if there is an underlying issue behind the behaviour, such as a learning support need resulting in the student feeling frustrated or bored, in which case it may be helpful to engage with the Educational Psychologist. Alternatively the pupil may be under stress or worry through a family situation: difficult emotions can manifest in several different ways and it can be useful to undertake some emotion work (see Chapter One) in such cases. The worksheets start with assessments of current situations and diagnostic tools to help identify the reasons for disaffection. They then move through activities to enable students to understand their misbehaviour and consider what part of their personalities can be helpful to change this and what skills need developing further. Behaviour is presented as a choice in these activities rather than an inevitability and as such, this approach combines cognitive-behavioural and solution-focused models.

Worksheets

Termly Self Assessment

This worksheet focuses on students investigating how they (rather than parents or teachers) want to change the situation in school. It is important that the ideas for change written here are fully from the student, rather than suggested by you, as this will make for better motivation to see it through. It is a beginning activity that can be referred back to during each term if things start to run off-course. It can also be used as an encouragement to show how much a student has managed to change his behaviour since the work began.

Log of Discipline Events

Every school will have their own consequences for poor behaviour, but this worksheet should be usable in any school situation. Sometimes poor behaviour can fall into patterns, which can easily be missed. This is one way to pull all that information together to spot whether there are more problems in any particular subject, or with any particular student. Sometimes a day of the week can stand out as being worse and specific reasons for these patterns can then be investigated.

It is important that this worksheet is not treated as a punitive measure, but rather as a neutral recording of information. A student will be less honest about her difficulties if she thinks this is a means of punishing her again. Specific targets with specific rewards can then be devised to combat specific problems.

Progress Record

This worksheet is designed to allow a student to compare his progress as weeks go by. It is designed to record both positive and negative consequences. The two columns before the bold line are intended for positive rewards, such as stickers, merits or house points, and the other columns are intended for the negative consequences, such as lines and detentions.

As with the previous worksheet, it is important not to be telling the student off for misdemeanours already punished, but praise can be given for positive rewards gained, especially if these can be seen to increase over time.

Score Your Lesson

There is deliberately no definition in this worksheet of the basis for scoring. This could be very individual, depending on the particular issues for each student. A student could score the lessons according to how well behaved he feels he is, or how much he chats to his friends, or how well he gets on with those particular teachers (if personalities are a problem). It is designed to be a snapshot of all the lessons, which can then be used to devise strategies to enable success in lessons currently viewed as very problematic. It is important that the student himself is free to put his own opinion down here.

It is always more effective to work with someone on something he perceives to be a problem. If he does not recognise a problem, then work needs to be done pre-behaviour change so that he sees that behaviour as problematic first. This tool can be used to compare the student's opinion to those of staff, so that glaring discrepancies can be spotted and addressed first.

I Misbehave in School Because...

Very often students who are aware of having behaviour problems will also know why it is happening. Sometimes this can be difficult for them to communicate. This worksheet is intended for use with a student who finds it difficult to express herself, or is not sure where the problem stems from. The results can give a good insight into some of the reasons, but also suggest some solutions. There are spaces for the student to write her own solution ideas. It starts to address the feeling of inevitability that often coincides with poor behaviour, suggesting that there is more than one way.

Why I Do Not Like School

This is a similar diagnostic tool to the previous sheet, encouraging the student to think about reasons for his behaviour. It does not take him on to the solutions yet, as he may not be at that stage. He may want to simply express some of his frustrations first.

SWOT Analysis

The SWOT (Strengths, Weaknesses, Opportunities and Threats) analysis is a preparation for the personal crest activity that follows. It starts to encourage the student to look at her own personal qualities. The 'Strengths' section is filled in with the things she feels she is good at and good qualities that make up her personality. A student will often start this section by being very school-orientated, naming subjects that she is good at, but try to encourage her to think about other aspects of her life too. The 'Weaknesses' section is filled with the areas she feels she is not good at and personal qualities that are not helpful. The 'Opportunities' section is for anything she does in or out of school that will give her skills and chances of doing different things. This can include clubs, hobbies, uniformed organisations, ambitions and interesting contacts. The 'Threats' section is filled with areas that are going to make it difficult for her to achieve and do well. This may include other people, tendencies to chatter in lessons or do silly things and could include family circumstances.

When summing up, end with a description of her strengths so that she can see all the positive things that are going to help her improve her current situation.

Personal Crest

Having completed the SWOT analysis, some of that information can form the basis of this crest. The crest can be completed in a number of ways, either as a whole picture to represent the student's image of himself or strengths, or it can be divided in two sections to show the difference between his positive and negative behaviours. Alternatively, the student can draw a cross in the crest to divide it in four sections and use each section to represent the SWOT categories from the previous exercise. This can be completed in any order, but now using pictures and symbols rather than words. The 'Opportunities' section could focus on future goals and dreams.

Imagination can be brought into play to decorate around the outside of the crest and a personal motto devised and written on the scroll.

Obstacles...and Their Solutions

Students will often cite reasons why they cannot change their behaviour, and this worksheet seeks to encourage them to come up with solutions to problems posed. If a student identifies an obstacle as difficulty working quietly in a lesson and always gets into trouble for chatting, he may say that a solution is to sit away from his friends. When this has been written down he then has a choice about whether he wants to use that solution or not. He is more likely to agree to use a solution if it is one he has come up with himself.

Personal Goals

Students are more likely to achieve and do well if they are in the habit of setting themselves personal goals over different time spans. This worksheet begins simply by focusing on the present but then introduces the idea of medium- and long-term goals. The statements on the worksheet can be discussed as a way to introduce the topic and gauge how much the student understands the significance of goal setting.

Who Has Control Over You?

Here the idea is introduced that control in situations can either lie within the student (internal) or with something the student cannot alter (external). Many students with behaviour difficulties will automatically externalise control for their behaviour, leaving them powerless to change it. An example of this might be that a student shouts at a teacher, and says that the teacher 'made' her do it by shouting at her first. If the student continues to think in that way, then she can never change the situation. If she realises that she has a choice over her own reaction to an incident, then she starts to internalise the control. She may not be able to change the original catalyst, but she can see reactions as a choice rather than an inevitability.

On this worksheet, there is one example to demonstrate to the student how it is to be used. It is worth noting that this sheet can also be used in a positive way to help students accept that they have done well. They may be tempted to always put their success down to external factors (for example, doing well in a test because it was easy anyway), whereas if they could internalise their achievement it would have a real impact on their self-esteem.

I Have a Choice

This activity is a development of internalising control. In the first column the student either draws or writes a description of an incident of poor behaviour on his part. In the second column he draws or writes what could have been a better choice of alternatives to practise thinking in that way, and then chooses the alternative he feels he would be most able to do in reality. Some role-play based on the second alternative may be a good support activity.

Thoughts/Feelings/Behaviour

This worksheet is a diagram of the cognitive-behavioural model, which states that our thoughts shape our feelings, which in turn shape our behaviour. The student writes an incident in the middle of the cycle, then writes in the appropriate place what her thoughts were at the catalyst stage of the incident. She then fills in the feelings that these thoughts induced (the Emotion Cards from Chapter One can be used if communication or vocabulary is limited). This then takes her to the behaviour area, where she fills in what she actually did in the circumstances. Having established a link between these three factors, the sheet can be redone, with the same catalyst, but this time altering her thoughts about that catalyst. She then needs to use her imagination to think what the knock-on effect of that change would have on the feelings and behaviour elements.

'I' Statements

Many students are getting into trouble over the way they speak to teachers, and are perceived as being rude. They find it difficult to express what they feel without appearing to be aggressive and challenging. Learning to use 'I' statements can be a method of assertively expressing what the problem is without putting blame onto the person being addressed. They always follow the same basic formula as follows: 'I feel...when...'

For example: 'I feel upset when you always think it is me who is talking', as opposed to: 'It's not fair. You always blame me whenever you hear anyone talking!'

The 'I' statement can be interpreted as being calm, non-blaming and clear in content. The other statement seems blaming, aggressive and angry.

This worksheet helps the student to look at common things that are said and to reword them as 'I' statements so they will be more constructive.

Obviously, 'I' statements are not a guarantee that the student will be listened to, but it does increase his chances. In order to help him do this in a real situation, some role-play may be useful.

Perfect Teacher/ Perfect Student

Many students have a very good idea in their heads already about what makes a good teacher. This worksheet is a way of encouraging a student to add to this picture attributes that make up the perfect student. She can then comment about how well teachers measure up, but also consider how she compares as well. She may be able to suggest specific areas for improvement from this.

Advise the Alien

This worksheet is devised to encourage the student to think about what skills are needed to survive in the classroom. Areas to look out for are listening skills, good memory, personal organisation, being prepared to have a go, good concentration and realising that they are probably not going to win an argument with a teacher!

Teachers Are Good/Not Good When They...

The students will already have a long list to fill the negative side of this sheet, but they are encouraged here to think of some positives as well. This helps some students who have an extremely negative view of all teachers.

What Can I/Teachers Do?

This is similar to the above sheet. Students will probably have a list of things teachers could do differently, but may miss the point that they themselves can make some alterations.

Positive Report Sheet

This sheet is a development of Bill Rogers' 'catch them being good' idea (Rogers, 2000). There are no negative comments allowed on the sheet, merely an acknowledgement of targets met. This has the dual purpose of encouraging students in what they are trying to improve and focusing teachers' attention on positive achievements and improvements, which may otherwise be overlooked.

Targets

This target sheet can be used both as an assessment tool and as a measure of improvement. It can be given to the specific staff that teach the student in question for them to comment. It has the advantage for teachers already pushed for time of being extremely quick and easy to complete.

Storytelling: The Arrogant Prince

As with all storytelling, try to 'tell' it rather than read it and allow the meaning to seep through by itself without explanation. The basic theme is of choice of behaviour being in the hands of each individual.

Activities

Self-portrait

This is another way of encouraging a student to look at themselves and who they are. It is useful to use with students who are not very communicative and those who enjoy creative work.

Give the student a piece of A3 card or paper. Ask her to draw a picture of herself in the middle. Then ask her to put all the things that represent different parts of her life or personality around her self-portrait. These could be people she is close to, things she enjoys doing, strengths she has, aspects of her personality, and things that are important to her.

This activity can be made as creative as you like, using coloured pens, collage materials and old magazine pictures.

Ask the student to talk you through her self-portrait, explaining why she has chosen to use each image.

Poor Listening Skills Role-play

Students tend to quite enjoy this, as it has an element of silliness about it, but it does convey the message in a memorable way. The student has to talk to you for two minutes about a subject of his choice and you have to role-play poor listening skills. This can include closed body language, looking at your watch, humming, biting nails, flicking things, looking all around the room and gazing out of the windows. The student will probably find it extremely difficult to actually keep talking! Explain what you were doing and ask him how it felt. Swap roles so that he has the chance to do the same to you! The objective is for the student to experience someone not paying attention. You can then link that idea to a classroom situation and how his inattentiveness affects the teacher.

Another direction to take is to ask the student what he remembers from when you were doing the speaking. The chances are he won't really remember anything! You can then make the link between paying attention and the retention of information, and that listening is not just passive.

Unseen Drawing

This exercise demonstrates graphically how difficult communication can sometimes be and how people can easily misunderstand what is being said.

Have some simple abstract line drawings already prepared on A4 paper and give the student a pen and blank paper. Sit back to back with the student and describe to her in words only how to draw the picture. The results will invariably be a different size to the original, and sometimes barely even resemble it! You can swap roles and repeat the exercise, giving her the frustration of working out how to communicate and how easily misunderstood her words can be.

This exercise is very effective if done in a group situation with students in pairs communicating different pictures.

Sequin-sorting

Many students find it very hard to comply with a teacher's request, as they do not understand why the task needs to be done in the first place. This is a very simple exercise that underlines the need for co-operation and self-control in school, even if the point of what they are being asked to do is not immediately obvious.

Put a small pile of assorted sequins in front of the student and ask him to sort them out into their separate colours. If he asks why, do not enlighten him at all but just repeat the instruction.

At the end of the task, explain that it was an entirely pointless job (as you replace them into one jar and mix them up!) but that he exhibited extremely good self-control in order to complete the task. Ask the student to tell you how the principle of what he did will help him in the classroom. (If he is stuck, point out that he often may not see the value or point of a task that a teacher has set, but that through sheer self-control he can get through it.) You can at this point give the student some small reward for completing the task, adding that he did not do it for that reward (as he did not know it was a possibility) but that sometimes rewards come simply through co-operation.

Helpful Contacts and Further Reading

www.publications.dcsf.gov.uk for a copy of Steer, A. (2009) *Learning Behaviour: Lessons Learned – A Review of Behaviour Standards and Practices in our Schools*. London: Home Office.

www.behaviour4learning.ac.uk

www.behaviourmanagement.org

www.incredibleyears.com

Rogers, B. (2009) *How to Manage Children's Challenging Behaviour*, second edition. London: Sage.

Termly Self Assessment

Term 1

What do I want to be different this term?

_____

_____

What do I want achieve this term?

_____

_____

_____

Term 2

What do I want to be different this term?

_____

_____

What do I want to achieve this term?

_____

_____

_____

Term 3

What do I want to be different this term?

_____

_____

What do I want to achieve this term?

_____

_____

_____

Term 4

What do I want to be different this term?

_____

_____

What do I want to achieve this term?

_____

_____

_____

Term 5

What do I want to be different this term?

_____

_____

What do I want to achieve this term?

_____

_____

Term 6

What do I want to be different this term?

_____

_____

What do I want to achieve this term?

_____

_____

Log of Discipline Events

Date	Subject	Comment

Progress Record

Date (week beginning) _____

Subject

English						
Maths						
Science						
Art						
P.E.						
I.C.T.						
French						
German						
R.E.						
History						
Tech.						
Geog.						
Drama						
Music						
P.S.H.C.E.						
Other						
Total						

The Learning Mentor's Resource Book

Student use | Chapter Ten: Behaviour Change

Photocopy or print from CD-ROM

10-16

Score Your Lesson

1 is the lowest mark, 10 the highest

Subject	1	2	3	4	5	6	7	8	9	10

I Misbehave in School Because...

☐ I hate school

☐ I want people to like me

☐ I don't like following rules

☐ The work is too easy

☐ I don't want people think I'm stupid

☐ I have trouble making friends with people

☐ I sit next to people who make me misbehave with them

☐ I don't like getting homework

☐ I get frustrated because I can't do the work

☐ The teachers pick on me

☐ I don't like teachers

☐ It's not fair

☐ I get bored

☐ I'm always in trouble anyway so I might as well

I Would Behave Well at School If...

☐ I could do the work

☐ It was fair

☐ It was more interesting

☐ There was no homework

☐ There were no teachers

☐ I had extra help

☐ I didn't have to_____

_____

☐ I had more friends

☐ The day was shorter

The Learning Mentor's Resource Book

Student use | Chapter Ten: Behaviour Change

Photocopy or print from CD-ROM

10-16

Why I Do Not Like School

The teacher picks on me.

I sit next to some-one I do not like.

The class is too noisy.

I find it too hard.

I need help but do not get any.

There's too much writing.

I always get into trouble.

I find it boring.

The teachers shout too much.

The teacher shouts at me a lot.

The work is too easy.

There's too much reading.

We get too much homework.

SWOT Analysis

Strengths

Weaknesses

Opportunities

Threats

The Learning Mentor's Resource Book

Student use | Chapter Ten: Behaviour Change

Photocopy or print from CD-ROM

12-15

Personal Crest

The Learning Mentor's Resource Book		
Student use	Chapter Ten: Behaviour Change	10-16
Photocopy or print from CD-ROM		

189

Obstacles...
and Their Solutions

Personal Goals

If you have no goals, that's exactly what you will achieve!

My goals for this week	My goals for the next year

My goals for when I leave school	My goals for when I am 30

To get anywhere, you must have a destination!

Who Has Control Over You?

Incident	Why	Control
I threw paper at a kid sitting behind me	He threw paper at me first so I had to throw it back	External

The Learning Mentor's Resource Book

Student use | Chapter Ten: Behaviour Change

Photocopy or print from CD-ROM

12-16

I Have a Choice

Thoughts/Feelings/Behaviour

Thoughts

Feelings

Behaviour

'I' Statements

Think about your areas of conflict.

Change the way you express what you feel into an 'I' statement.

Area of conflict	'I' statement

Perfect Teacher/Perfect Student

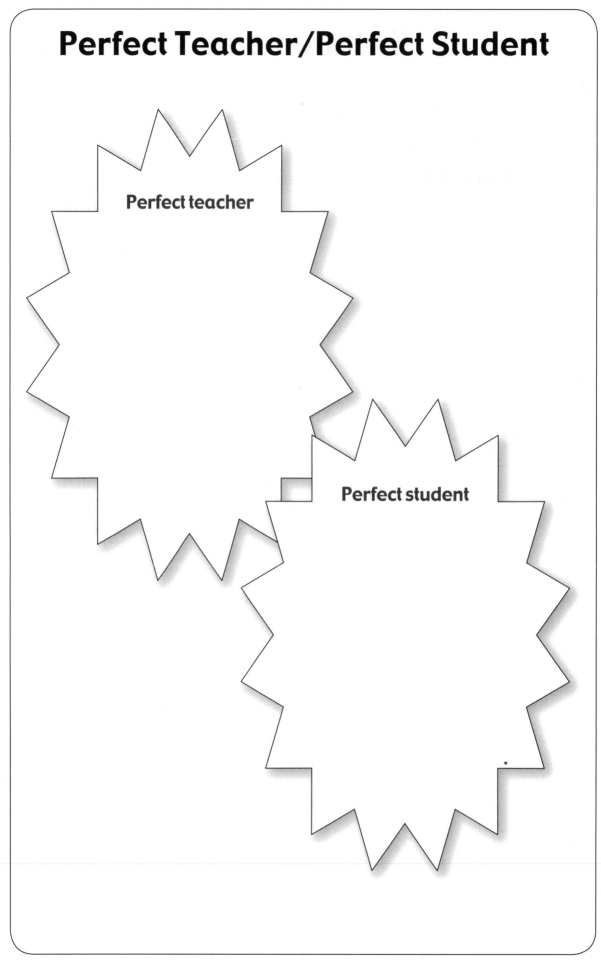

Perfect teacher

Perfect student

Advise the Alien

Think of ten things an alien would need to know to survive at school.

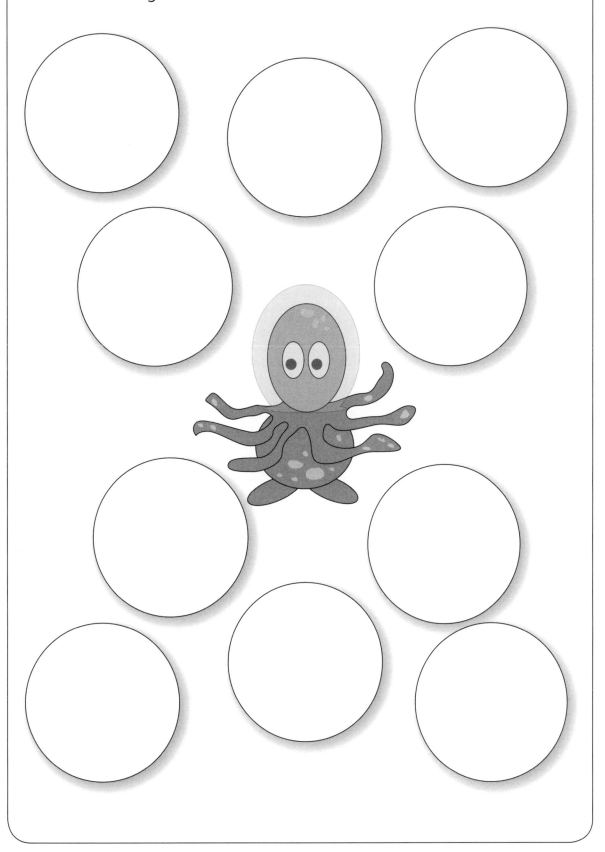

Teachers Are Good/ Not Good When They

Teachers are
good when they

Teachers are
not good when
they

What Can I/Teachers Do?

What can teachers do to make school a better place for me?

What can I do to make school a better place for me?

Positive Report Sheet

To staff: _____ has got a positive report sheet. Please will you initial next to the targets _____ has achieved in your lesson. Do not write any negative comments! If in doubt, please leave blank!

Targets: 1. _____

2. _____

3. _____

	1	2	3	4	5
Monday	1. _____ 2. _____ 3. _____	1. _____ 2. _____ 3. _____	1. _____ 2. _____ 3. _____	1. _____ 2. _____ 3. _____	1. _____ 2. _____ 3. _____
Tuesday	1. _____ 2. _____ 3. _____	1. _____ 2. _____ 3. _____	1. _____ 2. _____ 3. _____	1. _____ 2. _____ 3. _____	1. _____ 2. _____ 3. _____
Wednesday	1. _____ 2. _____ 3. _____	1. _____ 2. _____ 3. _____	1. _____ 2. _____ 3. _____	1. _____ 2. _____ 3. _____	1. _____ 2. _____ 3. _____
Thursday	1. _____ 2. _____ 3. _____	1. _____ 2. _____ 3. _____	1. _____ 2. _____ 3. _____	1. _____ 2. _____ 3. _____	1. _____ 2. _____ 3. _____
Friday	1. _____ 2. _____ 3. _____	1. _____ 2. _____ 3. _____	1. _____ 2. _____ 3. _____	1. _____ 2. _____ 3. _____	1. _____ 2. _____ 3. _____

The Learning Mentor's Resource Book

Facilitator use | Chapter Ten: Behaviour Change

Photocopy or print from CD-ROM

!

Targets

_____ has identified the following targets for this term. Could you indicate where you feel they lie on the 1–10 scale (1 being poor, 10 being great).

Target	1	2	3	4	5	6	7	8	9	10

Please could you put this in_____
when completed.
Thanks.

The Arrogant Prince

There was once a Prince who was incredibly arrogant. He thought he knew it all and had to answer to no-one. Now his father the King was very old and no longer able to make decisions, so he had entrusted all the important decisions to his wise counsel. The Prince was very jealous of this wise man and thought that he himself ought to be making the decisions, now that the King was old. The wise man was too wise to argue with the Prince and calmly went on with the day-to-day running of the country.

Eventually the Prince decided that the only way out of this situation was to plot to have the wise man executed. One day, he caught in his hands one of the beautiful but tiny little birds that lived in the palace gardens. He had the wise man brought into his presence and set him a challenge.

'Wise man, if you are wise enough to be making my father's decisions for him, answer me one question correctly, or you will be beheaded. I have here in my hands a tiny bird from the garden. Tell me whether this bird is alive or dead.'

The wise man considered the question. He knew that the Prince was cruel and also that he would do anything to gain power. He knew that if he said the bird was alive, the Prince would crush it in his hands to prove it to be dead. If he said it was dead, then the Prince would let it go to prove him wrong. There seemed no right answer.

After thinking about this for a few minutes, the wise man said: 'The answer, oh Prince, is in you hands.'

Chapter Eleven
TRANSITION

Introduction

For adults, starting a new job can be an anxious time. The transition for children from primary school to secondary is even more daunting. Equally, it can be an exciting opportunity to develop: meeting new people and learning new skills. The most commonly held fears are getting lost, being bullied and finding the work too hard (and having your head flushed down the toilet, something more likely in *Tom Brown's Schooldays*!). Despite these anxieties most students will accomplish a positive transition but some will encounter difficulties, which can escalate if not addressed. There should be a policy in each school regarding working towards a successful transition and there are many activities that can be done in support of this.

Secondary school staff should liaise with core staff at each primary school prior to the transition to prepare the students, hosting events such as visits and open days. The liaison should also identify vulnerable students who will require extra support, those with issues varying from learning needs or behaviour difficulties, to poor social skills. Individual support from the secondary school mentor could be offered for the student about whom there are acute concerns. This may involve sessions both at the primary and secondary school to address these concerns and prepare the student for secondary school. This support should be sustained at secondary school until the student has successfully settled in.

Individual students, who are making the transition from non-feeder schools, or those arriving in groups of two or three, may also benefit from extra support. This can be tackled by inviting such students to a 'transition session' to address any fears and provide an opportunity to meet others in the same situation. Introduce yourself as a source of help if there are problems on their arrival – past experience has shown how successful such transition sessions are in alleviating anxiety. Ideas for the content are included later in this chapter.

Obviously, transition involves a vast number of students. A support network could be established with the creation of 'buddies' for the new intake. This requires close liaison with either the Head of Year 7 or the transition team. Suitable volunteers should be recruited from Years 8 to 11, and groups of three to four assigned to each form. You may find it beneficial to appoint a 'head buddy' in each group, possibly an older student. The buddies would need training, ideas for which are provided, and accessible support. It is suggested that the buddies visit the allocated form during registration twice during the first week and weekly for a set period beyond that. This identifies the buddies as a support mechanism to deal with any problems that the new intake may be experiencing in the initial months; however, the buddies must understand that serious issues must be immediately referred to a learning mentor.

Worksheets

Each sheet should be worked through in a session with the student so that you can explore any issues.

Moving On Up!

This is simply here to use if you would like to make the following worksheets into a booklet for the student to keep. Alternatively, the student could design his own.

Your Thoughts...

This presents an opportunity for the student to express her thoughts regarding the positive and negative aspects about leaving primary school. Alternatively, you could use the 'Two Trees' exercise in the 'Transition Session' later in this chapter.

Your Thoughts... Secondary

The same exercise as above but regarding beginning secondary school. This gives you the opportunity to discuss any anxieties and to reinforce positive thoughts.

My Journey

The student can draw his journey to school whether it is a map of the route he will walk or a map to where he will catch the bus. It could be a picture of the bus the student plans to catch, including the bus number. The section 'What do you need to know about getting there?' focuses on factors such as how long the walk will take, which bus stop, what number bus, how much the bus fare is, what to do if running late and so on. This prompts preparation.

My School Bag

This aims to encourage organisation and awareness of the differences of secondary school. Help the students to consider the different books, equipment and homework they may need as well as necessities such as lunch, money, locker key, pens and a timetable.

My School Uniform

Some primary schools may not have a formal code of dress. Most secondary schools do, so it is important to help the student recognise the importance of wearing the uniform correctly. Some schools are very strict on their uniform policy. Ask the student to draw her new uniform. This should include rules about jewellery and any code of dress for sport.

My Equipment

Again this reinforces preparation. Ask the student to draw or write a list of equipment that will be needed. If you have the timetable, you could run through each lesson, specifying what equipment is needed. This should include the basics such as pens, pencils, ruler and timetable as well as specific items for each lesson, such as an apron for technology and a calculator for maths. Many schools provide a planner or diary for their students, which is vital for every school day, often carrying quite punitive punishments if forgotten. If this is the case, ensure the student understands how important it is that he remembers it.

Planning

Secondary school is a major change compared to primary school which may overwhelm the student. It is important to establish a routine from day one such as packing a school bag. You could also look at a homework timetable but this is difficult to predict prior to actually beginning the lessons; more general tips may be of use. You could add things here that may be of significance to the particular student.

What Happens If...

This provides the chance to stimulate the student's problem-solving skills. Allow the student to try and think of solutions himself but give advice if he struggles. This is to prepare for any such issues arising. The blank options are there for the student to suggest worries of his own, which you can then offer guidance on.

Very Important Things

Each school is different and places priority on varying aspects. All schools should place importance on attendance and punctuality, which should be explained to the student even if this is apparent at primary level. Make sure that the student is aware of any school discipline in the 'school rules' section. This allows you to cover any areas specific to your school.

Ideas for a Transition Session

Two Trees

Create two large trees, one an autumn tree and one a summer tree. Lay the two trees in the middle of the circle and have glue sticks available. The autumn tree represents primary school. Cut out yellow leaves on to which the students can write something sad about leaving primary school. On brown leaves, the students can write a good thing about moving on. They then stick all the leaves on the autumn tree. The summer tree represents high school; create red apples, cut out from coloured card, for the students to write on a worry about starting secondary school, and green apples for things they are looking forward to. Give each student two of each. Once completed, they stick the apples on the summer tree. Discuss the answers as a group. The worries about starting secondary school should be discussed thoroughly, coming up with ideas on how to combat these fears as a group. For example, a main anxiety is getting lost and solutions could be to ask a teacher, go to a point of help such as a student office or stick with your classmates.

Treasure Hunt

Create a set of directions following a set route around school. Create a second set of directions that follow the same route but in the opposite direction. After each direction ask a question, for example: 'Turn right out of Room 1 and follow the corridor. At the end there is a flight of stairs. What lesson is taught in the rooms at the top of the stairs?' Split the group in two, each with a facilitator. Give each group a different set of instructions – the winners are the first group back with the right answers. This activity should hopefully give an introduction to finding the way around the school and encourage interaction between the students.

Worry Wall

This has similarities to the Two Trees exercise and can be used in addition to it. Stick up a big sheet of paper entitled 'Worry Wall' and hand out a few post-it notes to each student. Ask the students to write a worry they have about starting secondary school and stick them on the Worry Wall. At the end of the session the group can discuss ideas to help relieve each worry.

Ideas for Buddy Training

Begin any training with icebreakers to mix the students (see bibliography for some books on this, although an internet search will provide a good variety of icebreakers!) and a 'Group Contract' to establish fair ground rules such as listening, confidentiality and having fun. The worksheets can be given out to each buddy in a booklet to use as a future source of reference.

My Own Experience

Ask each buddy to complete this individually and then discuss with a partner. This should help the buddies remember what starting secondary school feels like, putting themselves in the new student's shoes. Discuss different experiences as a group, creating a list of fears and what helped to resolve them. Hopefully this will inspire some thought about what will help the new intake, which is the theme of the following task.

Brainstorm of Ideas

Split the group into sub-groups according to the form in which they are allocated. In these sub-groups, the task is to create a list of ideas of what they can do to assist the transition of the form. Share ideas back in the whole group.

Active Listening

The facilitators should role-play an example of poor body language and then poor verbal skills. Ask the group to point out what was wrong in each scenario. Then explain what active listening is. You may find it helpful to use FELOR (see sheet) and demonstrate what this means.

The facilitators could then role-play examples of the following listening skills – reflecting, summarising and clarifying. Give the students some scenarios to practice this in pairs. Alternatively, this can work in groups of three with the third person as the observer, highlighting positives and improvements.

Feedback as a whole group as to how the exercise felt.

Some Useful Responses When Listening

This is a reference sheet to remind buddies of helpful phrases they can use.

What is Bullying?

An issue frequently brought to buddies by new Year 7 students is bullying so it is useful to prepare them for this. See Chapter Seven for more information.

Form Time Ideas

This provides suggested activities the buddies can use when spending time with their allocated form. It may be necessary for the buddies to meet with the form tutor to discuss what he feels is appropriate for his form.

Action Plan for Form 7

This is intended to turn everything the buddies have discussed into a plan of action. This may begin with the next time the buddies will meet and what they plan to do in their first meeting with their form.

Looking After Yourself

This should be used to explain confidentiality to the group. Buddies are intended to act as a support mechanism for the first few months, to deal with issues such as getting lost and making friends. It is not appropriate for buddies to deal with disclosures on more difficult issues such as problems at home or low self-esteem. Ensure the buddies are fully aware of this and to whom they should pass on information should this happen. This should also be clear to the new form groups. Buddies are expected to keep any problems brought to them as confidential with regard to their friends, but are encouraged to discuss the matter privately with a mentor, or fellow buddy, for guidance.

Buddy Scheme Training

This worksheet is an example of how a session could run. In any group work it is always advisable to start with icebreaker activities and to break up tasks with short games. There are quite a few included in this session plan as one aim of the session is to encourage the students to interact and mix with other students. Ensure you have back-up activities in case you have extra time. The 'Who' column refers to which facilitator will lead each activity.

Remember to provide access for support beyond the training. A member of staff on the transition team may wish to arrange regular meetings to supervise progress.

Helpful Contacts and Further Reading

http://nationalstrategies.standards.dcsf.gov.uk/transferandtransition

Alexander, J. (2004) *Going Up!: The No-worries Guide to Secondary School*. London: A&C Black.

Potter, M. (2009) *Moving On Up: All You Need to Ease the Transition from Primary to Secondary School*. London: A&C Black.

Moving On Up!

My name _____

My old school

My new school

Your Thoughts...

What are the good things about leaving primary school?

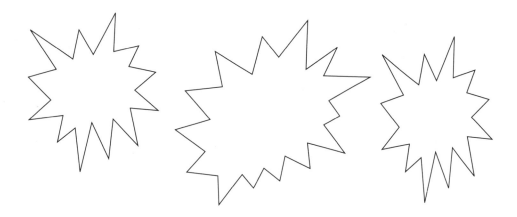

What are the hard things about leaving primary school?

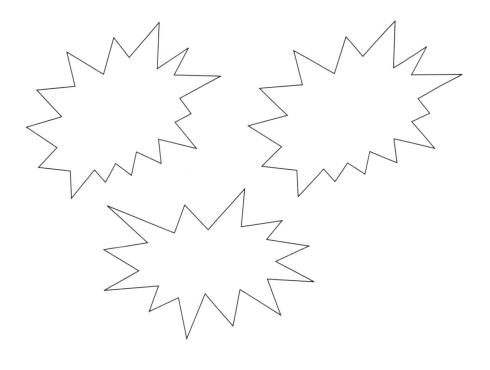

Your Thoughts... Secondary

What are the good things about starting secondary school?

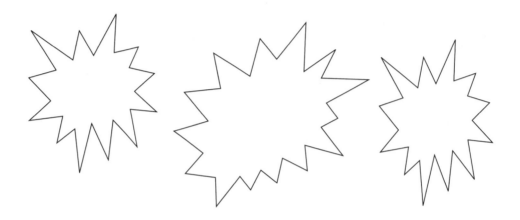

What are the hard things about starting secondary school?

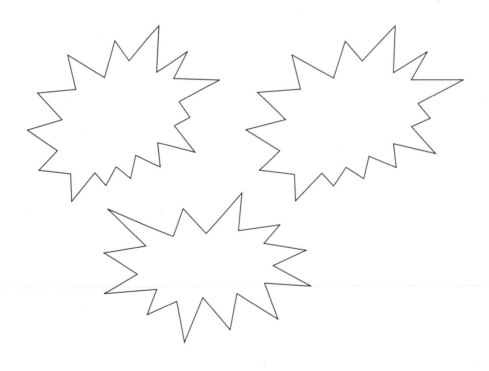

The Learning Mentor's Resource Book

Student use   Chapter Eleven: Transition

Photocopy or print from CD-ROM

10-11

My Journey

Draw a picture to show how you will get there.

What do you need to know about getting there?

My School Bag

At secondary school, there are lots of new lessons and you move to different rooms for each class. So it is important to have a school bag to carry your things in.

Draw what you might want to put in your school bag.

The Learning Mentor's Resource Book

Student use | Chapter Eleven: Transition

Photocopy or print from CD-ROM

10-11

My School Uniform

It is important to look smart at school. Make sure you are wearing the right uniform.

Draw the uniform for your new school.

My Equipment

Think about the different things you might need at your new school. What books will you need? What do you think you might have to wear for P.E.?

Write draw your ideas here.

Planning

It is a good idea to pack your bag the night before, so that you make sure you have everything you need – equipment, books and homework. Look at your timetable for help.

Draw a picture of you packing your school bag.

What Happens If...

I get lost?

_____

_____

_____

I forget my homework?

_____

_____

_____

I am ill?

_____

_____

_____

I need the toilet?

_____

_____

_____

Very Important Things

Punctuality...

_____
_____
_____
_____

Attendance...

_____
_____
_____
_____

Our School Rules...

_____
_____
_____
_____
_____
_____

The Learning Mentor's Resource Book		
Student use	Chapter Eleven: Transition	10-11
Photocopy or print from CD-ROM		

217

My Own Experience

Think about the first day you came to this secondary school.

What were you worried about before you started?

What was hard about your first couple of days?

What did other students do to help?

What did staff do to help?

Brainstorm of Ideas

What can form buddies do to make life easier for the new Year 7s?

Active Listening

Active listening shows the speaker that you are paying attention, and encourages them to open up and talk more.

This can be broken down into:

- Body language

- Verbal – what you say

Body language

Remember the following things!

Face the person

Eye contact

Lean forward

Open posture

Relax

Verbal

You need to make sure you have accurately heard what the person is telling you.

You can do this by...

1. Reflecting – you 'reflect back' (or repeat) what the person has just said. You may do this by saying: 'So what you're saying is …' or 'You feel… because…'

2. Summarising – if the person has had a long tale to tell, you can remember the main points to repeat back. You are trying to pick up on their keywords, thoughts or feelings.

3. Clarifying – check which the person that what you've understood is correct. You might say: 'Am I right in thinking…?'

The Learning Mentor's Resource Book

Student use | Chapter Eleven: Transition

Photocopy or print from CD-ROM

10-11

Some Useful Responses When Listening

Starting with phrases such as these will help you to encourage the person to talk.

'Sounds like... _____

'Seems as if... _____

'I hear you saying... _____

'I wonder if... _____

'I imagine... _____

'I think I hear... _____

'What I seem to be hearing... _____

'I get the feeling... _____

'Sounds to me like..._____

'Am I right in thinking... _____

'You seem to be... _____

'So you are feeling... _____

What is Bullying?

- Someone deliberately makes someone else feel miserable, or threatens them.

- Bullying causes the victim to feel frightened and unhappy.

There are different types of bullying...

Verbal – using hurtful words.

Physical – actually pushing, hitting, shoving, kicking.

Silent – could be ignoring someone, and trying to stop others talking to them.

Emotional – making someone else feel stupid, picking up on differences.

Did you know...

Four out of ten young people report having been bullied.

Form Time Ideas

Ask all the students to write down on a piece of paper one thing that they have found difficult.
Take back the papers and then hand them out again but make sure no one gets their own.
Go round the class. Each student reads out the problem and offers a solution to it.

Ask the students to form pairs and chat to their partner for two minutes, finding out two interesting facts about them. Then, going round the room, each person has to introduce their partner to the rest of the class.

This is similar to the previous idea, except the point is to find two things the partners have in common, then they introduce themselves by name and both say the things they have in common.

Around the room, each person should complete the sentence: 'If I were an animal, I would be...'

All students move around the room shaking hands with everyone and saying one fact about themselves... giving time for the other person to do likewise!

Make a word search, may be using words about high school.

You could start to look at student's attitudes by asking them to stand up if they agree with the statement you read out.

This could start with things such as:

- Stand up if you don't like wearing school uniform.

- Stand up if you like eating chips.

- Stand up if you watch Coronation Street.

  and could go on to things like:

- Stand up if you thinking bullying is wrong.

- Stand up if you have ever been bullied (be careful with this one!).

- Stand up if you think students should have more say in how the school is run...

You could add an extra dimension to this by getting everyone standing to swap places with someone else who is standing at the same time, mixing people up!

Try to help students to think how they are feeling, by asking each person to complete the sentence: 'My name is... and I feel...today.' Make sure you start this with the buddies themselves.

- You could do a brainstorm on the whiteboard on subjects like: 'What is bullying?'

- Each person in the room introduces themselves by saying their name and a describing word beginning with the same letter, for example: 'Hello, I am Perfect Peter,' 'Hello, I am Anxious Abigail.'

- Go round the room, making up a story, with each student adding just one line to it. So you may start by saying: 'There was once a boy called Henry.' The next person may add: 'He had a dog named Patch,' and so on! See where it ends up!

Remember: The form teacher is there to help you!

The Learning Mentor's Resource Book		
Student use	Chapter Eleven: Transition	12-16
Photocopy or print from CD-ROM		

223

Action Plan for Form 7

What we will do:

_____
_____
_____
_____
_____

How we will do it:

_____
_____
_____
_____
_____

Who will do what?

_____
_____
_____
_____
_____

How will we evaluate what we have done?

_____
_____
_____
_____
_____

The Learning Mentor's Resource Book

Student use   Chapter Eleven: Transition

Photocopy or print from CD-ROM

10-11

Looking After Yourself

Remember...

If someone tells you something that has happened in school, do not keep it to yourself!
You do not have to bear their burden on your own!
Always pass on the information (recorded on the record slip) to a learning mentor, who will then decide how it is to be dealt with.
The new students will know that nothing can be kept confidential if they tell you – they are reporting the incident if they tell you.
However, please ensure that you don't talk about what has been said to your friends...it is confidential from them. You may want to chat over something that has been said if it makes you feel uncomfortable, but please ensure that it is with a Learning Mentor.
The children will quickly become disillusioned if the information they are passing on to you becomes common knowledge through your friends.
You can always refer students to the peer listeners if you think they need someone to talk to.

Buddy Scheme Training

Exercise	Details	Items needed	Time	Who
Game/round	Play Fruit Salad to mix the group up. To play, all participants (including facilitators) sit round, in a circle, on chairs. Three types of fruit are chosen by the pupils and allocated one to each person, so everyone has a fruit name. One facilitator takes her chair out of the circle and stands in the middle as the first 'caller'. She calls one of the fruit, and each person with that fruit name has to swap seats with someone else. The caller has to leap into a vacant seat before it is taken. Hopefully this will result in a new caller who calls another fruit. The caller may call, 'Fruit salad,' if they wish, causing all players to have to find a different seat. Introductions game – in twos, each pair chats for a couple of minutes to find out two things they both have in common. They share their names and the two facts with the whole group.			
Aims	Hand out booklets. Go through and explain that it's a working booklet to be used today and kept for reference. Contract – brainstorm what should be on the group contract for the session to make it safe.	Booklets Pens Contract sheet Marker		
Ideas brainstorm	Brainstorm ideas for ways buddies can help new year 7s on a large piece of paper. All write up the responses in individual booklets.	Brainstorm sheet Markers Booklets Pens		

Own experience	In twos, discuss and complete the 'My Own Experience' sheet. Share with whole group one thing from each section (or pass).	Booklets Pens		
What will help	In groups, explore what the buddies can do to help the Year 7s. Referring to form time ideas, the buddies should think about what they will do with their form. Can share ideas as a whole group.	Booklets Pens		
Looking after yourself; Help pathways	As a group, brainstorm what issues the buddies should refer to a mentor. As a group, map out the referral pathways of who can help on a large piece of paper. Discuss confidentiality – the role of the buddy, what issues should be passed on.	Large paper ×2 Markers Booklets Pens		
Listening skills	Leaders role-play • bad body language • bad verbal skills Ask the group to say each time what was wrong. Go through and explain FELOR.			
Listening skills 2	Leaders explain and role-play each of the following one by one: • reflecting • summarising • clarifying			

Student practice	Students role-play in pairs from groups to practise the skills just explained (using the booklet for reference as needed) with one person being either: • a new Year 7 who is upset because he hasn't made any friends yet Or • a new Year 7 who is upset because someone has called him a name Swap over after a few minutes, so both of the pairs play both positions.	✏		
Feedback	How did that feel? Get general feedback. If necessary, pass a speaking object round the room with each person offering one thought about the experience.	Speaking object		
Summarise	Go through the other information in the booklet.	Booklets		
Action Plan	In the form groups, decide and create an action plan of what the buddies will do next – meetings with form tutor, introductions to form, what this will include, when etc.			
End game	Throw the ball around saying your own name and a feeling you are feeling now.	Ball		

Chapter Twelve
ATTENDANCE AND PUNCTUALITY

Introduction

School attendance has been a focal point of education reform for a number of years now. The government recommends that all children of compulsory school age should have a minimum of 95% attendance (Department for Children, Schools and Families). Many students fall well short of that and for many different reasons, some more legitimate than others. Previously, school attendance was seen as an 'education welfare' concern but now its concern has moved to attendance improvement and the more controversial enforcement approach with examples of parents being fined, made subject to Community Orders and even jailed for failing to ensure their child attends school.

For pastoral staff to try and address attendance, it needs to be ascertained *why* the student has poor school attendance and then work can begin on tackling the cause; for those students who are truanting because they do not want to come to school, work needs to be centred on motivational factors. The recent development of more vocational pathways within education may be explored as part of this. The worksheets based on goal setting from the behaviour section (Chapter Ten) may be transferable to attendance in such cases. Should the root cause relate to bullying, it may be useful to visit Chapter Seven.

Similarly, poor punctuality can also cause large chunks of schooling to be missed. Often problems are organisational, especially if the student comes from a rather chaotic family or has a diagnosis such as dyspraxia. As such, sometimes the cause of a student's lateness is beyond his immediate control and he may need help to address this.

However, the reason for school non-attendance may include more complex situations and needs to be uncovered so that appropriate support can be put in place. Engaging the family and making them aware of the importance of good school attendance is integral, as the family environment could be part of the problem. For example, the pupil may be a carer for someone else in the family, maybe even a parent, or in more chaotic households, a referral may be needed to a service such as a Family Intervention Project, parenting programme, support group or children's centre, who help with parenting support if there is a child in the household under five years old. It would seem that a more systemic approach to school attendance is important, working with the individual student, families and school staff. For parents who are trying hard to promote school attendance, they can feel judged and demotivated if their efforts go unrecognised and are ultimately met with enforcement action so this requires a fine balancing act by pastoral staff. It is hoped that this introduction will promote systemic thinking while the following worksheets and activities can be used with the student. The approaches found useful in dealing with attendance include solution-focused, motivational interviewing and cognitive-behavioural therapy.

Worksheets

Yearly Attendance Record

This sheet is a way to record attendance over a year. It can clearly be seen how the target setting can work on a half-term basis. Have a blank version to photocopy for use. Rewards can be given to students achieving their targets and then tighter targets set for the next half term. The form is deliberately dateless, so it can be used in any academic year. It is a very good way to keep a watch on attendance and punctuality, and a clear way for the student to see how well she is doing. Copies can be sent home for parents or carers to see both if a student is doing well, and if she is slipping and needs to be 'pulled up' about it. It has a space both for the week number and date. Different schools follow different ways of recording, so it is hopefully flexible enough to meet all demands in every situation.

Why I Do Not Come to School

There are lots of reasons listed here for school non-attendance. Don't be worried that they will give ideas to a school truant. If they are already missing school then there is already a reason for it. Some of these reasons are more emotive or embarrassing, so will be harder to admit to. This is where your relationship with the student is extremely important. On this worksheet, the student marks the reasons on the sheet that apply to him. It may be worth discussing confidentiality with him, as related issues may crop up. It may be a sheet that is worth revisiting after working with the student for a while. Some boxes have been left blank for the student to offer reasons not covered on this sheet.

What are the Consequences?

This helps the student to look beyond the here and now to more of the knock-on effects of his attendance problems. It also starts to look for a solution to his most common excuse for non-attendance.

The student puts his most common excuse or reason from the previous sheet in the 'Reason' box. In the next box, working down, he thinks of a short-term consequence (maybe within the next few months) of that situation continuing, and in the box after that he thinks of a long-term consequence (maybe within the next year or so). In the thought cloud above the 'Reason' box, he writes a solution to the problem that is stopping him go to school. If he cannot think of anything, then you may need to discuss options with him, but it is always more effective if a young person comes up with his own solutions. This is repeated for up to three different reasons for truanting.

Box of Reasons/Problems

This is a useful place to start with a student who appears to be not attending merely because he doesn't want to. He is truanting because he has no motivation to come to school. This is designed to focus his mind on the purpose of coming to school and to move away from the idea that he is doing someone a favour by attending. It is making the costs and benefits very personal and looking to find motivation from that. You could develop the idea by creating an actual box with items in to represent each cost and benefit.

Attendance Reward Card

The attendance reward card is a way of finding motivation for de-motivated students to come to school. It is used in conjunction with stickers, which are freely available from many outlets. Stickers can motivate a surprisingly large age range of students, right up to the end of Key Stage 3 (age 14). There are many ways this card could be used, but one idea is to put a small sticker on a symbol for each day attended (the lines of sticker spaces do not necessarily relate to complete weeks), and a large sticker on a smiley face for each full week attended. It can be used in conjunction with the attendance record chart and it helps to remind students with attendance difficulties (in a nice way) that someone is watching!

Attendance Letter

Included in this section is a sample letter, which could be sent home to parents or carers of students with attendance difficulties, to underline that the school is very worried about their child's attendance. It could be altered in any way appropriate and is just one example of how parents or carers could be included in the process.

Reasons and Excuses

Similar to the Why I Do Not Come to School worksheet, this is a diagnostic tool to help uncover the reasons for a student's persistent lateness. The student again marks the reasons she considers most account for her lateness, and adds others of her own if necessary.

Reasons and Excuses (Part Two)

This worksheet follows on from the previous sheet. The student chooses from her selection on the first sheet the two she feels are the most frequent reasons for her being late (there may only be one reason that happens consistently, so in that case only one part of this worksheet is filled in). The reason is written in the top half of the box, including any secondary reasons (for example, she may always sleep in because she is playing computer games until late at night). In the bottom part of the box, she writes a solution to the problem. She can write more than one solution if she can think of them, and then choose one she would like to work on. The sheet can then be re-visited after a week to see if there has been any impact on punctuality, and the outcomes of the changes made written in the 'Outcome' box.

My Day Before School

If organisational issues are seen to be at the heart of the lateness, then running through all the different things that have to be done before school and analysing how long they all take will help. It can be seen whether it is all logistically possible considering what time the student gets up and what time she has to be in school. It is remarkable how often the student is not leaving herself enough time to complete all the activities she sets herself. It can then be clearly demonstrated that the lateness will not improve unless she gets up earlier, completes her tasks faster or misses out non-essential things. The first times to be put in are the time she gets up and the time she needs to be in school. There is a gap left between leaving for school and arriving at school, as distractions along the way may be the culprit.

Helpful Contacts and Further Reading

www.dyspraxiafoundation.co.uk

www.direct.gov.uk/en/Parents/Schoolslearninganddevelopment/YourChildsWelfareAtSchool

Franklin, F., Harris, M. B. and Allen-Meares, P. (2008) *The School Practitioner's Concise Companion to Preventing Drop Out and Attendance.* Oxford: Oxford University Press.

Yearly Attendance Record

Week No.	Date week commencing	M	T	W	T	F	Target	Week No.	Date week commencing	M	T	W	T	F	Target

Key:

/\	present all day	O	truancy
/	present am	L	late
\	present pm	X	training day
E	exclusion	H	holiday
I	ill	•	end of school year

232

The Learning Mentor's Resource Book
Facilitator use | Chapter Twelve: Attendance & Punctuality
Photocopy or print from CD-ROM

Why I Do Not Come to School

I have to babysit.

I have to help a member of my family.

I don't like school.

I forgot to do _____ so I will be in trouble if I come to school.

There's no point coming to school, as I'll do badly anyway.

I have been threatened by _____ so I am too scared to come to school.

My mum wanted me to go shopping with her.

Someone has to stay at home with the dog.

I'm too worried to leave _____ at home to come to school.

School is boring – I have much better things to do.

I have _____ which means I am often too ill for school.

_____ happens at school, which makes me not want to come.

The Learning Mentor's Resource Book		
Student use	Chapter Twelve: Attendance & Punctuality	10-16
Photocopy or print from CD-ROM		

233

What are the Consequences?

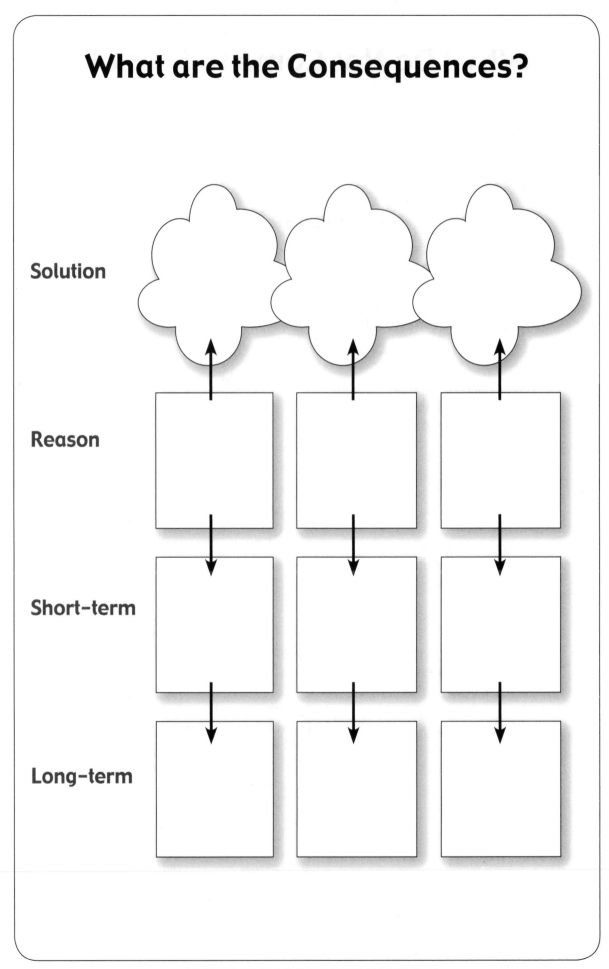

Solution

Reason

Short-term

Long-term

Box of Reasons/Problems

Box of reasons to come to school

Box of problems if I do not come to school

The Learning Mentor's Resource Book		
Student use	Chapter Twelve: Attendance & Punctuality	
Photocopy or print from CD-ROM		

10-16

235

Attendance Reward Card

Attendance Letter

XYZ School,

_____

_____

_____

Date.

Ms _____

_____

_____

_____

Dear _____
I am writing to you to express concern about your child's attendance.
Having checked the registers recently, the Head of Year and myself
have found that _____'s attendance is _____%.
We are worried about this because_____ is missing a lot of
school, and may
find it hard to keep up with classmates. The government does
recommend that all children should attend school for at least 95% of
the time, and you can see that _____'s attendance is much
lower than that.
I do appreciate that there may be difficulties preventing regular
attendance and will
be available at school to discuss this with you. I hope that by writing to
you about
this, we will be able to work together to help_____ come to
school more regularly.
The Attendance Improvement Officer may have to become involved if
we cannot improve _____'s attendance.

Yours,

| The Learning Mentor's Resource Book | ! |
| Facilitator use | Chapter Twelve: Attendance & Punctuality |
| Photocopy or print from CD-ROM |

237

Reasons and Excuses

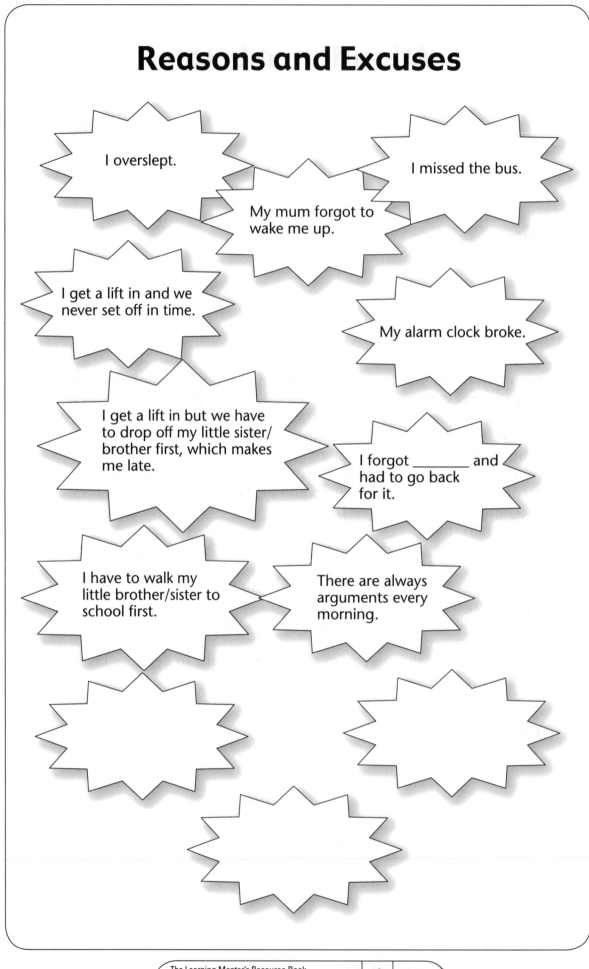

I overslept.

I missed the bus.

My mum forgot to wake me up.

I get a lift in and we never set off in time.

My alarm clock broke.

I get a lift in but we have to drop off my little sister/brother first, which makes me late.

I forgot _____ and had to go back for it.

I have to walk my little brother/sister to school first.

There are always arguments every morning.

The Learning Mentor's Resource Book

Student use | Chapter Twelve: Attendance & Punctuality

Photocopy or print from CD-ROM

10-16

Reasons and Excuses (Part Two)

Choose your two most relevant reasons for being late:

Reason	Reason
Solution	**Solution**
Outcome	**Outcome**

My Day Before School

Time started		How long?	Time finished
	Get up		
	Leave for school		
	Arrive at school		

Chapter Thirteen
SCHOOL REFUSAL AND ANXIETY

Introduction

School refusal can occur for wide-ranging reasons. Sometimes the student has always had separation anxieties, sometimes there are issues the school needs to address such as bullying, but sometimes it can be an apparently irrational fear of school. Students may be able to say what they are feeling (if they have the vocabulary – the Emotion Cards from Chapter One can help here), but they may have no idea why they feel this way. It seems almost as if school has become a scary monster that they just cannot face anymore.

It is important to acknowledge the way a student feels, and if this is what she is saying, advice to contact her GP may be useful. However, it is not necessarily indicative of some sort of mental health problem and can be dealt with in a highly controlled de-sensitisation programme. If mental health professionals are involved, then obviously their advice should be sought as to the appropriateness of getting the student back into school.

Worksheets and Activities

When Do You Feel Most Anxious At School?

This can be a useful audit of the circumstances that could possibly cause anxiety during the school day. It may help identify particular factors that school can directly address so that the student no longer needs to have anxiety in that area.

Answers to this worksheet can provide direct ways forward and suggestions for solutions. If the student either cannot answer the questions, or wants to tick all the boxes, then it is likely that school is falling into the 'scary monster' category above for him.

I Don't Like School Because...

This provides another way to pinpoint some of the times and places about which a student may feel anxious. It would be helpful to use this in a situation where the student is reluctant to talk or offer any reasons himself. There are concrete suggestions to be offered to him, which merely require a yes or no answer. This could be a nod or a shake of the head!

Why I Like/Do Not Like School

This encourages the student to think about very specific reasons as to why she does not like school. It also, very importantly, encourages her to find some aspects that are positive, even if it is just the bell at the end of the school day!

Scaling

Ask the student to rate himself from 0 to 10 as to how anxious he feels about school. Explain that '0' is as anxious as anyone could possibly be and '10' is not anxious at all. Mark this position, with the date, on the scaling sheet.

It is extremely rare for anyone to rate themselves as '0'. Say, for example, the student responds with '2'. The next question could be to ask him what makes it as high as '2'. The next aim is to encourage the student to think about positives, so follow up with a question asking what have to be different for him to rate himself as '3'. Encourage him to think of very small improvement.

The scalling sheet can be used in this way at each meeting to map out the student's level of anxiety. He will be encouraged to increased the number nominated if he spots that some of the improvements discussed at the previous session have happened in the intervening time.

The worksheet can be used almost universally in all areas of difficulty, merely changing the subject of the question being asked.

The Ladder

This worksheet is designed to map out a plan for reintegration of a student who is refusing to come into school, but could also be used in conjunction with the scaling sheet to write down the improvements that happen which nudge her up the scale. Each rung can either represent a level on the scale, with the improvements written in between, or it could represent each meeting, with the rungs being coloured in if the improvements have been happening.

For serious school refusers, this worksheet was designed to show the tiny steps they need to take in order to get back into school. For someone who refuses even to set foot into school, the first rung could be to come to school and meet you at the school gates, then go home again. This can be progressed to coming and meeting you in school somewhere, and slowly extending time spent in school by minutes if necessary. The ladder would be the result of a meeting between you and the student (and possibly parents or carers) to map out all the stages to be progressed through. It is recommended not to write up too many at once, maybe just four or five rungs; otherwise the student could become fearful. Each time a rung has been achieved, the student could colour the ladder up to that shape and receive a sticker on the footprints, or whatever reward she would value.

Obviously, all reintegration programmes need to be agreed by appropriate staff in school, but this method can often break what seems to be a deadlock of refusal.

Draw the Obstacle

Explain to the student that there seems to be some obstacle in the way of them being able to come to school. Use his own words to explain that something is scaring him and stopping him attending. Ask the student to draw a picture of himself at one end of a piece of paper, then ask him to draw a picture of school at the other end. Now (without any explanation of what it could be) ask him to draw the obstacle that is standing between himself and school. If he is struggling, simply ask him to use his imagination to think what it might look like. Once there is something on paper, ask him why he cannot walk past it. What is it doing? What is it about it that makes it so scary?

Turning something ethereal into something concrete makes it easier for students to discuss.

Scary School Monster

In some ways this is similar to the 'obstacle' exercise above, but it uses more imagery to begin with. You could tell a short story about people being scared by a big monster that turns out to be pretending to be what it isn't (*The Three Billy Goats Gruff* is a good story for this). Then explain the imagery of school seeming like a scary monster that the student does not dare to approach. Ask the student to draw the school monster, name it, and then the fear can be talked about in a more metaphorical way, centred on the monster that has been drawn.

Storytelling: The Frightened Lion

Telling stories can be very therapeutic and little, if any, explanation is needed at the end. Leave the student to mull over the story himself. As with all good storytelling, it is most effective if told rather than read.

Anxiety Stoppers

The anger management section worksheet 'Putting Out the Flame' can be adapted to use with students suffering from the anxiety that can lead to school refusal. By changing all references of 'anger' and 'angry' to 'anxiety' and 'anxious', it can be photocopied and made into a set of cards in the same way.

Helpful Contacts and Further Reading

www.handsonscotland.co.uk/topics/anxiety/school_refusal.html

www.schoolrefuser.org.uk

Heyne, D. and Rollings, S. (2002) *School Refusal (Parent, Adolescent and Child Training Skills)*. Oxford: WileyBlackwell.

Thambirajah, M.S., Grandison, K. and De-Hayes, L. (2007) *Understanding School Refusal: A Handbook for Professionals in Education, Health and Social Care*. London: Jessica Kingsley.

When Do You Feel Most Anxious at School?

☐ Catching the bus   ☐ Before school

☐ Registration   ☐ Assembly

☐ Lesson time   ☐ Changing lessons

☐ Lunchtime   ☐ Going into lunch

☐ After school

When being asked to:

☐ Write something down   ☐ Ask a question

☐ Answer a question (out loud)   ☐ Put your hand up

☐ Do something physical   ☐ Go into small groups

☐ Read out loud   ☐ Read quietly

☐ Do a test   ☐ Get the results of a test

In particular subjects

Subject	Because of teacher	Because of subject
P.E.		
Maths		
English		
Science		
Geography		
History		
P.S.H.C.E.		
R.E.		
Art		
Music		
German		
French		

Put a star against the five most difficult areas.

I Don't Like School Because...

I find _____ difficult.

I always get picked last at games.

I find maths difficult.

I find geography hard.

I find art hard.

I don't have many friends.

I find history hard.

I find English difficult.

I find French difficult.

I find German difficult.

I find science difficult.

I get blamed unfairly.

The teachers don't like me.

I get most of my work wrong.

I don't like P.E.

It makes me angry.

My test marks are always the lowest.

It makes me scared.

It's too big.

I don't like the way I look.

I get picked on.

I find it hard to read in class.

I'm lonely.

I find it hard to listen.

I find it hard to make friends.

I find it hard to concentrate.

I find it hard to keep up with the writing.

Why I Like/Do Not Like School

I like school
because...

I do not like
school
because...

The Learning Mentor's Resource Book

Student use | Chapter Thirteen: School Refusal & Anxiety

Photocopy or print from CD-ROM

10-16

Scaling

0 is as anxious as anyone could possibly be
10 is not anxious at all

(0) (1) (2) (3) (4) (5) (6) (7) (8) (9) (10)

The Learning Mentor's Resource Book
Student use | Chapter Thirteen: School Refusal & Anxiety
Photocopy or print from CD-ROM

10-16

247

The Ladder

The Learning Mentor's Resource Book

Student use | Chapter Thirteen: School Refusal & Anxiety

Photocopy or print from CD-ROM

10-16

The Frightened Lion

There was once a lion living in a jungle. He looked like a very fierce lion and had a incredibly handsome mane. He used to wander around roaring. All of the other animals were scared of him because he seemed so fierce. But Lion had a terrible secret. He wasn't very brave at all. In fact, you could say he was a real scaredy-cat! And what was he most scared of? Other lions!

Now this was OK most of the time, but recently it had been getting very warm and the stream where Lion always drank from had just dried up. This meant he was going to have to go and drink from the lake at the other end of the jungle. In this lake lived the fiercest lion ever known. Lion knew this because he had seen him – just once – when he had tried to get a drink. As he bent down, the other lion's awful face had appeared and looked as if he were about to eat him up! Lion had run for his life as fast as he could, never to return.

Lion looked in vain for somewhere else to drink, but eventually got so desperate that he knew he was going to have to go to the lake.

'Maybe if I creep up very quietly he won't hear me and I'll be safe', thought Lion to himself as he looked longingly at the glistening water. He circled round, padding softly on huge paws, looking for his moment to take a delicious drink. With a thumping heart, he crept to the edge of the water and peered over. Oh no! There was the other lion, waiting for him, looking as fierce as a lion could look. Lion dashed away from the edge and sat under a tree feeing more and more desperate.

Eventually, knowing he would die anyway if he did not get a drink, Lion crawled back to the water. His dry mouth told him he had no choice but to face the other lion. Looking into the fearsome eyes of the other lion, Lion plunged his head into the cool water and…the other lion disappeared.

Chapter Fourteen
REVISION

Introduction

This chapter is not an exhaustive list of revision techniques but more a guide to direct students who may be struggling with revision.

Successful revision starts well in advance of exams. If a student requires support with organisational skills, help him to devise a 'To Do' sheet or list. This could be designed on a computer and expanded to cover all subjects. Alternatively, a revision timetable can be beneficial; a template is included. This can be useful for those students who are more capable but experience anxiety. Students will find different support mechanisms useful depending upon their level and learning style. The student may be encouraged to understand their own learning style and whether this is visual, aural or kinesthetic.

It is important to remember that the brain concentrates for approximately 20–30 minutes so it is advisable to revise in short blocks with mini-breaks in between. This could involve making a drink, listening to a favourite song or having a chat with someone. However, this should only last around five minutes! The idea is to do something different from revision. The brain also remembers information more efficiently with use of colour or pictures.

Revision and exam time can be stressful for young people so allocating some time for relaxation is vital. This may be playing sport, spending time with friends or family, watching TV, relaxing in a bath or listening to music.

It is worth investigating which steps your school is taking toward support with revision techniques. Some schools invite local agencies to present study skills workshops. If this is not offered, it may be an avenue to explore.

Worksheets and Activities

Revision Planner

This template can be used whichever way the student finds beneficial. The idea is to use one timetable per week. The student initially blocks in times when she is unable to revise such as school hours, any work activities or training commitments for sport or hobbies. The student could colour this in one colour and entitle it 'busy time' or similar. The timetable is more successful if the student is realistic, therefore she should plot in times when she knows she has planned recreational activities, for example, going to the cinema or a family birthday. The student could colour all this in a second colour naming it 'My Time' or similar. The left over time slots should be, in theory, available revision time – substantial time must be dedicated to revision. This may mean the student is required to make sacrifices such as not watching as much TV or sleeping late at the weekend! A recommended idea is to colour each subject a specific colour and plot blocks in. The student can chose to entitle the subject, such as 'Maths', or with a sub-topic, e.g., 'Fractions'. It is worth allocating more time slots to subjects that the student finds difficult, and consider which exams are imminent. Try blocking in a time slot of an hour per subject, with one or two mini-breaks.

Revision Techniques Booklet

These worksheets are intended for use as a booklet, given to the student with the aim of providing different revision techniques. It is important to consider that every individual has a different learning style and ability. From supporting the student you may have an idea of this, enabling you to steer her in the right direction. It is suggested that you read through each technique with the student to discuss how to put it into practice and discuss any concerns.

Helpful Contacts and Further Reading

www.bbc.co.uk/schools/revision

www.bbc.co.uk/schools/gcsebitesize

www.s-cool.co.uk

www.projectgcse.co.uk

www.learning-styles-online.com

Cottrell, S. (2008) *The Study Skills Handbook*, third edition. Basingstoke: Palgrave Macmillan.

Davis, D., Sirotowitz, S. and Parker, H. P. (1996) *Study Strategies Made Easy: A Practical Plan for School*. Champaign, IL: Research Press.

Revision Planner

	Mon	Tues	Wed	Thurs	Fri	Sat	Sun
9am							
10am							
11am							
12pm							
1pm							
2pm							
3pm							
4pm							
5pm							
6pm							
7pm							
8pm							
9pm							

Week:_____

The Learning Mentor's Resource Book

Student use | Chapter Fourteen: Revision

Photocopy or print from CD-ROM

14-16

Revision Techniques

For successful revision...

Be confident, believe in yourself, get organised!

Remember...

Give yourself some time to relax and chill out.

Setting

It is best to sit at a table or desk where it is quiet and you are not distracted or disturbed. Make sure you have good light and you are warm.

If you prefer to listen to music as you revise, don't let it be too loud or distracting!

Breaks

It is very important to take lots of breaks. If you revised solidly for two or three hours your brain would only remember the first 20 minutes! So break from your revision every 30–45 minutes or whatever you find works best for you.

Break for five minutes and think of something totally different – turn your music up, play a favourite song, watch some TV, read a book or magazine, have a drink or something to eat.

Organisation

Revise in advance! It is best to revise topics more than once. First, revise the subjects for which the exams are earliest, or in which you struggle.

- Make 'To do'/Tick lists
  i.e. Biology   – Photosynthesis
                 – Reproduction
                 – Digestion system

- Make and use revision timetables

Equipment

You'll need pens, pencils, school books, any info/text books, coloured pens, plain/lined/scrap paper, blue-tack, any subject equipment, folder(s) to keep notes in.

1. Note taking

Make them colourful! Your brain likes colour.

Use short sentences and abbreviate – so long as it makes sense to you.

Just note the key information.

Make one set of neat notes then rewrite them out a few times in scrap. Then try turning your notes over so you can't see them and write down everything you can remember.

When you compare this to your neat notes add on what you have forgotten in a different colour.

2. Highlighting

If you have any printed sheets of notes or your own textbooks (you can't highlight the school's, they'll want them back for other students!), one idea is to get some different coloured highlighters or felt tips and highlight the important information – the essential parts!

Highlight information that is new to you. It will stand out to your eye but don't highlight everything!

3. Mind mapping

One idea is to map out what you already know. You can add to your maps whenever you learn something new. These work well as they connect information fast and store lots of info.

Here's how to do it...

- Use blank, white paper and turn it sideways (landscape).

- Put your key word of the topic you are revising in the middle. Use colours!

- Put the main topics on the thicker 'branches' coming from the middle.

- On smaller thinner branches coming from these words, write the smaller subtopics and details.

- Draw symbols or pictures near the words as your brain remembers pictures better than words.

- You could then circle or use a question mark next to areas you are unsure about and need to come back to.

- If you need to rewrite or redraw these maps, that's fine! This can help the information stick in your head.

- You can also use them to map out what you are learning as you revise. You could try making some more detailed notes, then map these out afterwards as a summary to look back on.

The Learning Mentor's Resource Book

Student use | Chapter Fourteen: Revision

Photocopy or print from CD-ROM

14-16

Why not display these maps as revision posters? (See Posters)

4. Acronyms

It sounds confusing, but this can be a useful way to remember important information on a topic. Use the first letters of the key words or names of the topic to create a word you will remember. For example, in Geography, the tectonic plates that float on the earth's mantle can be put into this order.

Africa

North America

Nazca

Antarctica

South America

Pacific

Indo-Australian

Eurasian

The first letters spell out ANNA'S PIE. This also reminds you there are eight pieces of information you need to know, as there are eight letters.

5. Rhymes

You could use the first letters of the key words or phrases to make up a funny rhyme to remember it by.

As an idea, the names of the planets in the solar system could make up this rhyme.

My	Mercury
Very	Venus
Energetic	Earth
Mother	Mars
Just	Jupiter
Swam	Saturn
Under (the)	Uranus
North	Neptune
Pole	Pluto

Again, you could stick these around your bedroom (if it's OK with your parent or carer!).

6. Questions

Being interested in a topic helps you to learn faster. Try asking the following questions about a topic to improve your understanding. Asking questions helps you concentrate better.

Who? How? When? Why? What? Where?

Let's show you an example…

If you were studying the Great Fire of London you may ask these questions:

WHO started it?
HOW far did it spread?
WHEN did it begin/finish?
WHAT happened afterwards?
WHY did it do so much damage?
WHERE did it start?

7. Posters

Create colourful posters about the key topics you are studying. You could write the topic across the centre of the page and write the essential information around it. You might want to add pictures or just use colours and highlighters. Or you could write the topic at the top of the page and have bullet points or a flowchart below.

This idea is to stick (with parent's or carers' permission) these posters in places you will see them often such as:

- bedroom walls
- your desk at home
- the back of cupboard door where you keep your favourite food
- the fridge door
- the back of the toilet door!
- next to your mirror
- near your stereo

Change your posters every few days so you are looking at new information or simply draw a picture or diagram that summarises the topic.

8. Practise exam questions/ papers

This one may sound a bit boring but it gets you into the practise of answering similar questions to what might appear in your actual GCSE. Your teacher may ask you to do some of these in class or as homework.

Practise makes perfect!

In subjects such as History and English, you could try essay plans. This is when you are given examples of possible essay questions you might be faced with in your exam, and you plan what your essay would say. Try brainstorming the title first to see what ideas and answers you come up with then revise over these areas. Write brief notes on what you would include in your introduction, main body and conclusion. Put page reference numbers to your texts where appropriate.

9. Test yourself!

After you have revised a topic, test yourself by closing all books and hiding all notes and seeing what you can remember. Say it aloud or jot it down. Then check back to your books. Or, ask a parent or friend to test you. They should have your notes or books and ask you questions. This is a good way to see your friends and revise on the run up to exams. You can help each other with parts that you are struggling with.

10. Physical revision!

If you find you learn better kinetically, that's to say physically, then try walking around your rooms as you read out your notes/books.

Get up and move about every 20–30 minutes

Act it out! Act the topic out in your bedroom or house. You could do this with a friend.

Remember to check back to your books.

Read out your notes in a dramatic or a funny voice. This is good if you learn better audibly.

11. Tape yourself

Another idea if you struggle to learn by writing things down is to read out the information that you need to learn to a tape recorder if you have one, and record it. You can then play it back to yourself as many times as you need to.

12. Key Words

Write a list of key words for the topic with no information and then tell yourself the details that belong to that key word. Or write these words onto flash cards and stick them about your room, then every time you see the key word recite all the information you can remember.

Everyone will have a different learning style so remember that different techniques might work for you compared to a friend!

It is important to revise for as much as possible – remember it is only for a few weeks or months of your life – however, do not stress yourself out. Have some relaxation time in between revising or before you go to bed. Get a good night's sleep before any exams.

13. Colour Maps

Use a certain colour for each subject or topic you are studying and write/draw all your information for that subject in the colour. Take the same colour pen into your exam for that subject as a visual link.

GOOD LUCK!!

Chapter Fifteen
FRIENDSHIP

Introduction

Many of the good times we experience are with friends – and a lot of the problems we experience come from friendship difficulties. Some students have difficulty in making or sustaining friendships. This can be especially hard in the transition from primary school to secondary and throughout high school, as children develop their individual identity, which can alter friendships. While some students may be happy to play alone, most of those without friends feel isolated and lonely. This causes a sense of rejection and even anger, which can then be displayed through their behaviour. Some students who lack confidence may exaggerate their behaviour to hide this and may seem dominating or aggressive. This can cause the student to appear as a bully.

Students who are good at establishing friendships are skilled communicators. They will generally have a good level of emotional empathy and are often confident in themselves. This therefore indicates that a student with poor friendship skills would benefit from improving his confidence and self-esteem, while addressing his emotional intelligence.

This section aims to develop the student's understanding of what friendship is and encourage strategies to help make friends. Friendship is a skill like any other that can be learned and improved.

Worksheets

Friendship Skills Basic Checklist

This can be used to provide a general idea of the student's strengths and weaknesses in his friendship skills. It therefore highlights where support is needed and which skills to concentrate on improving.

Friendship is…

Drawing is often an effective, non-personal method of expressing thoughts and is also very useful if the student finds talking difficult, whether due to low ability or just discomfort. This worksheet is for the student to draw what she thinks friendship is. It is important to allow the student to explore this herself rather than instructing her what to draw. You can then ask her to tell you about the drawing. This leaves the response very open. The student may write her response if preferred.

Draw What Makes a Bad Friend

This allows the student to draw images of his perception of a bad friend. Again this allows a very free scope and this should be maintained when asking the student about his drawing. The suggested response is: 'Tell me about this picture.'

Draw What Makes a Good Friend

As above, but focusing upon good friendships.

A Bad Friend

This worksheet aims to help the student identify poor friendships. There are two ways in which you may use this. It can be used to support the student's awareness of poor friendships that others are providing. Ask her to think about a particular friend and then circle the behaviours this friend displays.

It is important that the student is aware that these are only signs of poor friendship if they happen on a regular basis, as opposed to once in an argument! You can then discuss with the student how these behaviours are not valuable to the friendship. The worksheet can also be used to help the student think about her own friendship skills in the same manner. You could use a fresh worksheet or circle in a different colour. This use of the worksheet is more relevant for a student who is demonstrating poor friendship skills: they may be domineering or deceitful. If the student is not at the stage where she is ready to identify these behaviours on this personal level, she can use the sheet to think about poor friendships generally.

A Good Friend

This worksheet has the same usage as the previous sheet, but it focuses upon friendship qualities.

It aims to help the student realise good aspects in a friendship and raise awareness of what strong friendships involve. It can also highlight what is missing in a poor friendship. The second use of this sheet is to encourage the student to think about his own qualities as a friend. This should either promote self-esteem or indicate which attributes need addressing, depending upon the student's issues.

How Good a Friend are You?

This quiz is intended to be a light-hearted and fun method of highlighting the student's personal strengths and weaknesses in friendship. You may wish to discuss any relevant points arising from the verdict.

Tackling Shyness

This worksheet supports those students who generally display good attributes as a potential friend but who are too shy to actually establish friendships. It is also useful for students who are nervous, have low confidence or are quiet. It simply provides some techniques for the student to try in order to overcome her shyness. These techniques work more efficiently if you are also working with the student on improving her confidence.

Friendship

This list provides ideas, from a group of 13-year-olds, on ways to make or not make friends. The student rates himself on the statements in the list that he feels apply to himself and, in the second half, looks at how to change some of the negative skills into more positive skills.

Top Tips for Making Friends

This worksheet reinforces the previous activity in providing different ideas for making friends. Go through each idea with the student; discuss what it means and how she could implement it, in relation to her particular issues. Ask the student how she could act upon the tips.

Friendship Circles

This sheet can be used once the student has established some friendships as a measure of his 'success', or it can be used to boost self-esteem if a student believes he has fewer friends than he actually does.

The idea is that in circle 1 the student writes the names or initials of those immediate people who are really close to him. This could include parents, carers, siblings, family and possibly a close friend. Circle 2 represents people such as good friends and other family members such as an auntie. Circle 3 is filled with other friends who the student knows reasonably well and is friendly with but are maybe not close to such as classmates, peers at a youth club, friends of the family, a sibling's friends. Acquaintances such as teachers, doctors, football team managers and next-door neighbours are placed in the last circle. This aims to show the student what friendships he does have and which are important.

Helpful Contacts and Further Reading

www.need2know.co.uk/relationships/friendship

www.youthgroupgames.co.uk/friendship-building-games.html

http://childlight.co.uk/friendship-issues

Friendship Skills Basic Checklist

Use this basic checklist as a guide to identifying those areas in which the student has strengths and weakness. This should highlight where the student requires support in improving particular skills.

Understanding

☐ Can he provide examples of what a friend is?

☐ Is he aware of ways to sustain a friendship?

☐ What is his awareness of the effects of not having friends?

Social skills

☐ Can he share personal property?

☐ Can he take turns in games?

☐ Does he understand and respect the concept of queuing?

☐ Does he use appropriate greetings?

☐ Is he aware of different manners in which to speak to people?

Emotional intelligence

☐ Can she describe emotions that are experienced in different situations, for example, parents arguing, going to the dentist, a pet dying?

☐ Can she identify different emotions from facial expressions?

☐ Can she read body language?

Role awareness

☐ Can she imagine herself 'in the other person's shoes'?

☐ Is she aware of the effect of her actions or behaviour on others?

☐ Can she tell a story from a different view?

☐ Does she understand that there is more than one side to a situation?

The Learning Mentor's Resource Book		!
Facilitator use	Chapter Fifteen: Friendship	
Photocopy or print from CD-ROM		

261

Friendship Is...

Draw What Makes a Bad Friend

Draw What Makes a Good Friend

The Learning Mentor's Resource Book

Student use | Chapter Fifteen: Friendship

Photocopy or print from CD-ROM

10-14

A Bad Friend

A Good Friend

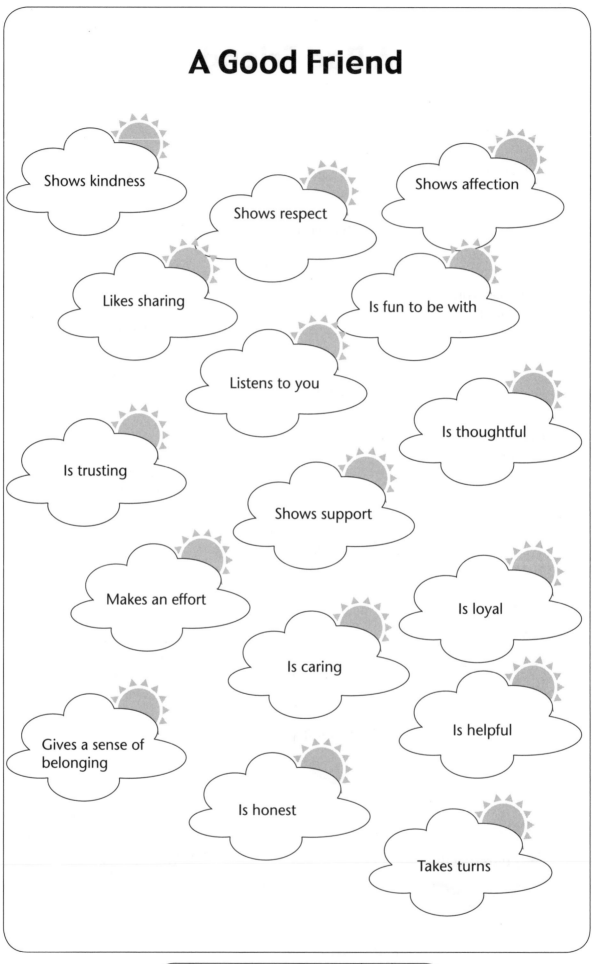

Shows kindness

Shows respect

Shows affection

Likes sharing

Is fun to be with

Listens to you

Is thoughtful

Is trusting

Shows support

Makes an effort

Is loyal

Is caring

Gives a sense of belonging

Is helpful

Is honest

Takes turns

How Good a Friend are You?

1. Which statement best describes you?
   - ☐ a. Very friendly
   - ☐ b. Fairly friendly
   - ☐ c. Not very friendly
   - ☐ d. Unfriendly

2. How easy do you find it to talk to people that you don't know?
   - ☐ a. Not very easy
   - ☐ b. Fairly easy
   - ☐ c. Very easy
   - ☐ d. Difficult

3. How easy do you find it to talk to new adults?
   - ☐ a. Difficult
   - ☐ b. Fairly easy
   - ☐ c. Not very easy
   - ☐ d. Very easy

4. How easy do you find it to talk to new kids?
   - ☐ a. Not very easy
   - ☐ b. Difficult
   - ☐ c. Fairly easy
   - ☐ d. Very easy

5. Which statement best describes you?
   - ☐ a. Easy going
   - ☐ b. Fairly easy going
   - ☐ c. Bad tempered
   - ☐ d. A bit touchy

6. A new student has joined your class, would you:
   - ☐ a. Make friends straightway
   - ☐ b. Wait to see whether you liked them
   - ☐ c. See whether other students like them
   - ☐ d. Ignore them

The Learning Mentor's Resource Book		
Student use	Chapter Fifteen: Friendship	10-14
Photocopy or print from CD-ROM		

267

How Good a Friend are You? (continued)

7. Your friend comes to school wearing terrible perfume/deodorant, would you:
   - ☐ a. Tell them it was not very nice, but in a gentle way
   - ☐ b. Tell them it's awful
   - ☐ c. Try not to notice it
   - ☐ d. Call them names like, 'Stinky!'

8. Your best friend gets a detention for something they didn't do, would you:
   - ☐ a. Shout at the teacher in their defence
   - ☐ b. Say nothing
   - ☐ c. Laugh at your friend
   - ☐ d. Tell your friend afterwards that you know they were in the right and you're sorry they got told off for nothing

9. You find your friend being called names by a group of older students, would you:
   - ☐ a. Run away
   - ☐ b. Try to help your friend
   - ☐ c. Call the bullies awful names back
   - ☐ d. Hang around until they'd gone before talking to your friend

10. You fall out with your friend over a misunderstanding, would you:
    - ☐ a. Smack them one
    - ☐ b. Try to make peace with them again by clearing up the misunderstanding
    - ☐ c. Not talk to them for a day
    - ☐ d. Spend time with other friends instead

11. What is most likely to make you and your friend fall out?
    - ☐ a. Believing rumours about something they have said
    - ☐ b. Not lending each other things
    - ☐ c. Not giving lent things back
    - ☐ d. Thinking they don't like you any more

12. What are you most likely to do immediately after falling out with your friend?
    - ☐ a. Cry
    - ☐ b. Try to make friends again
    - ☐ c. Hit them
    - ☐ d. Tell other people things about them

The Learning Mentor's Resource Book

Student use   Chapter Fifteen: Friendship

Photocopy or print from CD-ROM

10-14

13. How much time do you spend with your friends when you're not in school?

☐ a. We're never apart

☐ b. Never see them outside school

☐ c. Most days

☐ d. Occasional times

14. If your friend asked you for money, would you:

☐ a. Refuse to lend them any

☐ b. Lend them whatever they wanted

☐ c. Think about it first

☐ d. Slag them off at the thought that you'd ever lend them money

15. Who is most likely to make the first move when you have fallen out with your friend?

☐ a. You

☐ b. Them

☐ c. Both of you

☐ d. Neither of you – you'd never be friends again!

Friendship Quiz – How to Total

Question no.   Total

Question no.					Total
1	A=4	B=3	C=2	D=1	
2	A=2	B=3	C=4	D=1	
3	A=1	B=3	C=2	D=4	
4	A=2	B=1	C=3	D=4	
5	A=4	B=3	C=1	D=2	
6	A=4	B=3	C=2	D=1	
7	A=4	B=2	C=3	D=1	
8	A=2	B=3	C=1	D=4	
9	A=1	B=4	C=3	D=2	
10	A=1	B=4	C=2	D=3	
11	A=1	B=2	C=3	D=4	
12	A=4	B=3	C=2	D=1	
13	A=4	B=1	C=3	D=2	
14	A=2	B=4	C=3	D=1	
15	A=4	B=2	C=3	D=1	
				Total	

What is your score?

Read the verdict about how good a friend you are!

Friendship Quiz – Verdicts

15–24

With friends like you, who needs enemies?

You can't admit you're wrong, or make the first move to sort out a fall-out. You need to be more forgiving!

You always assume that others are getting at you and you don't feel secure in your friendships at all. You tend to assume that you won't like people you've never met before – try to be a bit friendlier to new faces!

Try to let things go a little bit without taking offence all the time and treat others as you would like to be treated. That way, you are more likely to keep the friends you have!

25–36

You need to be careful! Your tendency to assume that others are in the wrong, rather that yourself, puts you at risk of losing your friendships. You are sometimes willing to sort out friendship problems, but not often enough!

People you don't know are not always people to avoid – try being braver with new faces!

Be more willing to forgive friends who wind you up. Remember that your true friends are not your enemies – they are on your side! Never be tempted to treat your friends badly – you may need them one day!

37–49

You are usually a good friend to others. You consider their needs as well as your own and try to treat them as you would want to be treated.

You will find it quite easy to make new friends and know how to keep the ones you already have. You have good, balanced relationships with others, not allowing yourself to be used, but also not using them.

Keep this attitude to others and you'll never be without a friend!

50–60

Wow! What a wonderful friend you must be! You really go the extra mile to show your friends that you care about them! You hate falling out with them and do everything you can to put the situation right.

You have a lovely, caring attitude to other people, but make sure you don't let people walk over you.

You are always willing to forgive for what others do, instead of taking offence.

Well done!

The Learning Mentor's Resource Book

Student use | Chapter Fifteen: Friendship

Photocopy or print from CD-ROM

10-14

Tackling Shyness

Feeling shy is a natural part of growing up. Even confident people feel shy sometimes!

Making new friends can be difficult when you are shy because you can seem quiet, or nervous or feel awkward.

Try these ideas to tackle feeling shy or improve your confidence...

1) Chill out!

Learn to relax. Feeling shy makes you feel anxious and tense.

Tense your toes together and hold for a few seconds. Then slowly relax them. Now tense your feet. Slowly relax them. Next, try tensing your legs and slowly relax them. Work your way through your whole body. Feel the difference in your muscles.

2) 7–11

Breathing quickly or in shallow breaths will make your heart beat a bit faster, which will make you feel more anxious! Breathe in slowly and deeply to the count of seven, then breathe out to the count of 11. This should help you feel calmer.

3) Focus your mind

When you are feeling nervous or shy, you will be thinking about what is going on inside of you. Focus your attention on what is going on around you. Notice all the small details surrounding you, where are you standing, who are you with, what colour jumper are they wearing. Give yourself a running description of the scene. This will hopefully distract your mind from how you feel inside!

4) Positive thinking

Trick yourself into believing that you aren't feeling shy! Tell yourself that there is no problem. Say short positive statements to yourself such as:

'I can do this.'

'Blushing is not a problem.'

'I am OK.'

Add some of you own...

_____

_____

5) Say something

If it is the first time you have met somebody, try saying something! The other person is likely to reply to you, which could start off your conversation. You could even say: 'I never know what to say when I first speak to someone!'

Other things to say could be...

_____

_____

_____

_____

_____

_____

Friendship

Quality	1	2	3	4	5	6
Show interest in what people do						
Good at giving compliments						
Have a pleasant expression						
Laugh at people's jokes						
Kind						
Ask, not demand, to join in						
Offer to help others						
Invite people to do things						
Hang around where other students are						
Welcoming to new students						
Good at thinking of interesting things to do						
Willing to share						
Humorous and tell jokes						
Fair						
Good at organizing games						
Bossy						
Tell others how to behave						
Tell others they are doing things wrong						
Talk about yourself a lot						
Mean						
Talk about other people behind their back						
Negative and sarcastic						
Too intense and serious						
Brag						
Moan a lot						
Bully						
Claim credit for things you didn't do						
Lie or cheat						

The Learning Mentor's Resource Book
Student use | Chapter Fifteen: Friendship
Photocopy or print from CD-ROM
10-14

Top Tips for Making Friends

- Smile.

- Be friendly and helpful.

- Talk to others at break and lunch time.

- Show an interest in other people's activities.

- Be kind.

- Try to change yourself rather than trying to change your friends.

- Practise listening to them – try not to interrupt! Make sure they have finished speaking before you begin.

- Ask questions to show you are interested and to make sure you understand.

- Practise giving your undivided attention when listening to a friend.

- Try to see situations from your friends' point of view as well as your own. Imagine how it would feel if you were in their shoes.

- When arguments happen, try to find a positive outcome that both of you are happy with. This means you will both have to compromise.

- Remember your friends do not 'belong' to you. Share your friends.

- Spend time with your friends. It is OK to have different friends, just make sure no one is left out.

- Show your trust in your friend by lending him things. When you borrow something from a friend, make sure you return it in the same condition it was – this shows your friend that you can be trusted.

- Be honest – lying about something will only hurt and anger your friend and you will lose her trust. Be honest with your feelings.

- If you have a problem with a friend, talk to them about it. Choose a suitable time and place, and discuss your feelings calmly. Listen to your friend's response.

Friendship Circles

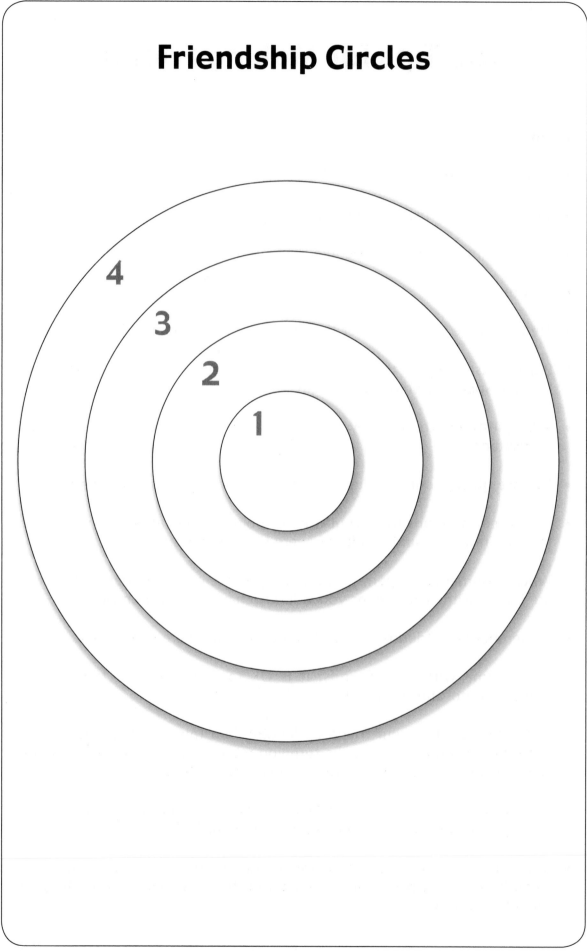

BIBLIOGRAPHY

Alexander, J. (2004) *Going Up!: The No-worries Guide to Secondary School.* London: A&C Black.

Alexander, J. (2006) *Bullies, Bigmouths and So-called Friends.* London: Hodder Children's Books.

Bailey, S. and Shooter, M. (2009) *The Young Mind.* London: Bantam Press.

Bar-On, R. and Parker, J. (2000) *The Handbook of Emotional Intelligence.* San Francisco: Jossey-Bass.

Browne, D., Clarke, S. and McCaffrey, T. (2003) *D'Fuse.* Leeds: Leeds Youth Offending Team.

Casey, J. (2002) *Getting it Right.* Bristol: Lucky Duck Publishing Ltd.

Cottrell, S. (2008) *The Study Skills Handbook*, third edition. Basingstoke: Palgrave Macmillan.

Davis, D., Sirotowitz, S. and Parker, H. P. (1996) *Study Strategies Made Easy: A Practical Plan for School.* Champaign, IL: Research Press.

De Shazer, S., Dolan, Y. and Korman, H. (2007) *More Than Miracles: The State of the Art of Solution-Focused Brief Therapy (Haworth Brief Therapy).* New York: Haworth Press.

Doel, M. and Marsh, P. (1992) *Task-Centred Social Work.* Hampshire: Ashgate Publishing Ltd.

Elliott, M. (1998) *Wise Guides – Bullying.* London: Hodder Children's Books.

Faupel, A., Herrick, E. and Sharp, P. (1998) *Anger Management.* London: David Fulton Publishers.

Fox, C. and Hawton, K. (2004) *Deliberate Self-Harm in Adolescence (Child and Adolescent Mental Health).* London: Jessica Kingsley Publishers.

Franklin, F., Harris, M. B. and Allen-Meares, P. (2008) *The School Practitioner's Concise Companion to Preventing Drop Out and Attendance.* Oxford: Oxford University Press.

Gersie, A. (1991) *Storymaking in Bereavement: Dragons Fight in the Meadow.* London: Jessica Kingsley Publishers.

George, S. (2009) *The Learning Mentor Manual.* London: Sage.

Goleman, D. (1995) *Emotional Intelligence: Why it Can Matter More Than IQ.* London: Bloomsbury.

Hampson, K. (2010) *Young People with Anti-Social Behaviours. Practical Resources for Professionals.* Oxford: Routledge.

Heegaard, M. (1991) *When Someone Very Special Dies.* Minneapolis: Fairview Press.

Heyne, D. and Rollings, S. (2002) *School Refusal (Parent, Adolescent and Child Training Skills).* Oxford: WileyBlackwell.

Home Office (2009) Hate Crime – The Cross-Government Action Plan. See: www.homeoffice.gov.uk/documents/hate-crime-action-plan

Honey, P. and Mumford, A. (1992) *The Manual of Learning Styles*, third edition. Berkshire: Peter Honey.

Holland, S. and Ward, C. (2002) *Assertiveness: a Practical Approach.* Oxon: Speechmark Publishing.

Johnston, S. (2002) *Is It Fair?* Bristol: Lucky Duck Publishing.

Kadushin, A. and Kadushin, G. (1997) *The Social Work Interview: A Guide for Human Service Professionals*, fourth edition. New York: Columbia University Press.

Long, R. (1999) *Friendships.* Tamworth: NASEN.

Lookadoo, J. (2008) *The Dirt on Drugs.* Revell: Michigan.

Maines, B. (2003) *Reading Faces and Learning About Human Emotions.* Bristol: Lucky Duck Publishing.

Marris, B. and Rae, T. (2004) *Escape from Exclusion.* Bristol: Lucky Duck Publishing.

Mayer, J. and Salovey, P. (1997) 'What is Emotional Intelligence?' In Salovey, P., Brackett, M. and Mayer, J. (eds) *Emotional Intelligence: Key Readings on the Mayer and Salovey Model.* Port Chester, NY: National Professional Resources.

Mental Health Foundation (2006) *Truth Hurts Report.* Free to download from: http://www.mental-health.org.uk

Miklowitz, G. (1986) *The War between the Classes.* New York: Random House. See www.randomhouse.com

Middleton, K. and Garvey, S. (2008) *Self Harm: The Path to Recovery.* Oxford: Lion Publishing Plc.

Miller, W. R. and Rollnick, S. (1991) *Motivational Interviewing: Preparing People to Change Addictive Behaviour.* New York: The Guilford Press.

McGuire, J. (2000) *Cognitive-Behavioural Approaches: An Introduction to Theory and Research.* HM Inspectorate of Probation. London: Home Office.

Moseley, J. and Sonnet, H. (2003) *101 Games for Social Skills.* Cambridge: LDA.

Moseley, J. and Sonnet, H. (2003) *101 Games for Self-esteem.* Cambridge: LDA.

Murray Parkes, C. (2006) *Love and Loss: the Roots of Grief and its Complications.* London: Routledge.

Plummer, D. (2007) *Helping Children to Build Self-Esteem: A Photocopiable Activities Book*, second edition. London: Jessica Kingsley Publishers.

Potter, M. (2009) *Moving On Up: All You Need to Ease the Transition from Primary to Secondary School.* London: A&C Black.

Prochaska, J., Norcross, J. and Diclemente, C. (1995) *Changing for Good.* New York: Perenial Currents.

Rae, T. and Johnson, P. (1999) *Crucial Skills.* Bristol: Lucky Duck Publishing.

Rae, T. (2000) *Confidence, Assertiveness, Self-esteem.* Bristol: Lucky Duck Publishing.

Rae, T. and Nelson, L. (2004) *Remembering.* Bristol: Lucky Duck Publishing.

Robinson, G. and Maines, B. (1998) *Circle Time Resources.* Bristol: Lucky Duck Publishing.

Robinson, G. and Maines, B. (1992) *The No Blame Approach.* Bristol: Lucky Duck Publishing.

Robinson, G. and Maines, B. (1997) *Crying for Help.* Bristol: Lucky Duck Publishing.

Rogers, B. (2009) *How to Manage Children's Challenging Behaviour*, second edition. London: Sage.

Rogers, B. (2000) *Behaviour Management – A Whole-School Approach.* London: Paul Chapman Publishers.

Salter Hampson, K. (2008) *Setting Up And Running A Peer Listening Scheme.* Oxford: Routledge.

Selekman, M. D. (2002) *Solution-Focused Therapy with Children: Harnessing Family Strengths for Systemic Change.* New York: Guilford.

Sheldon, B. (1995) *Cognitive-Behavioural Therapy.* London: Routledge.

Smith, C. (2002) *B.E.S.T. Buddies.* Bristol: Lucky Duck Publishing.

Spandler, H. and Warner, S. (2007) *Beyond Fear and Control: Working with Young People Who Self Harm.* Ross-on-Wye: PCCS Books Ltd.

Spotlight: Promoting Emotional and Social Development, issue 1, December 2003. National Children's Bureau: London.

Stacey, H. and Robinson, P. (1997) *Let's Mediate.* Bristol: Lucky Duck Publishing.

Thambirajah, M. S., Grandison, K. and De-Hayes, L. (2007) *Understanding School Refusal: A Handbook for Professionals in Education, Health and Social Care.* London: Jessica Kingsley.

Thompson, N (2006) *Anti-Discriminatory Practice*, fourth edition. Basingstoke: Palgrave Macmillan.

Wardle, C. and Rae, T. (2002) *School Survival.* Bristol: Lucky Duck Publishing.

Williams, E. and Barlow, R. (2001) *Anger Control Training.* Bicester: Speechmark Publishing Ltd.

Worden, J. W. (2002) *Children and Grief: When a Parent Dies.* New York: The Guilford Press.